BASIC BIBLE SERIES

ACTS

POWERED BY THE SPIRIT

DAVID C. COOK PUBLISHING CO.
ELGIN, IL 60120

Acts: Powered by the Spirit

© 1986 David C. Cook Publishing Co., 850 North Grove Ave., Elgin, IL 60120. Printed in U.S.A.

Scripture quotations, unless otherwise noted, are taken from the Holy Bible: New International Version, © 1973, 1978, 1984 by the International Bible Society, used by permission of Zondervan Bible Publishers.

Design: Melanie Lawson
Cover: Dale Gottlieb
Compiled by: Cynthia Schaible Boyll
Edited by: Gary Wilde

ISBN: 0-89191-519-2
Library of Congress Catalog Number: 86-70886

Acts 1:8

You will receive power . . .
and you will be my witnesses.

Contents

1
Come, Holy Spirit

Truth to Apply: Jesus prepares me, as His disciple, for the tasks He wants me to do.

Key Verse: But you will receive power when the Holy Spirit comes on you; and you will be my witnesses in Jerusalem, and in all Judea and Samaria, and to the ends of the earth (Acts 1:8).

J. I. Packer writes in *Keep in Step with the Spirit*, ". . . those who have thought about and sought after the power of the Spirit in their own lives have regularly found what they were seeking, for in such cases our generous God does not suspend his blessing . . . [until we get the] details of theology all correct. Conversely, where the Spirit's ministry arouses no interest and other preoccupations rule our minds, the quest for life in the Spirit is likely to be neglected, too. Then the church will lapse, as in many quarters it has lapsed already, into either the formal routines of Christian Pharisaism or the spiritual counterpart of sleeping sickness, or maybe a blend of both."

What is your personal experience with the power of the Holy Spirit? Do you agree, or disagree with Packer's comments?

Background/Overview: *Acts 1:1—2:13*

This passage bursts forth with the refreshing message that the Holy Spirit is with us and in us. If your life is suffering from spiritual doldrums and you sense some meagerness in your understanding of the Holy Spirit, then meditating on the following text should help. Before beginning this study, ask God, "Open my eyes that I may see wonderful things in your law" (Ps. 119:18).

Light on the Text

1:1   The author of Acts is Luke, the same evangelist, doctor, and companion of Paul who wrote the third gospel (see Col. 4:14; Philem. 24; and II Tim. 4:11). Similarities between Luke 1:1-4 and this verse serve to make the connection between Luke's account of Christ's life, death, and resurrection and Luke's history of the early church.

For example, in both Luke and Acts the recipient of Luke's writing is Theophilus. Since no other reliable source exists to connect this name with any known early church figure in history, some commentators have speculated that Theophilus, meaning "friend of God," is a literary device. In Luke's Gospel, however, he is referred to specifically as *"most excellent* Theophilus," giving credibility to the view that he was a real person.

1:2, 3   Verses 1-3 introduce the principal players of Acts. First, Luke points to Jesus, whose miracles and teachings he covers in the third gospel. Now he mentions how Jesus showed Himself to the disciples after His resurrection to strengthen their faith, and how He spoke to them about the Kingdom of God, helping them understand the significance of the Gospel.

Second, Luke emphasizes the apostles. They had been handpicked by Jesus and were the primary witnesses to His resurrection appearances. Verse 13 leaves no doubt who they are. This list corresponds with Luke 6:14-16; Mark 3:16-19; and Matthew 10:2-4.

Third, the Holy Spirit comes onto the stage of Luke's narrative as the central figure of the book. The Spirit has empowered Jesus' witness to the disciples. Now, in turn, the Spirit is promised to the disciples for their witness to the world. Sometimes Acts is rightly called "The Acts of the Holy Spirit" as well as "The Acts of the Apostles."

1:4, 5   In this command, Jesus' concern is that the disciples wait to witness until they are properly empowered. To emphasize their need of the Holy Spirit, He draws a parallel between their ministry and His own by reminding them of John the Baptist's prophecy (Mt. 3:11). Jesus had received the special gift of the Spirit when He began His own ministry. The disciples also need this gift to be effective.

1:6   From our perspective, the question of Jesus' followers may seem incredible. Jesus reminds them of the coming of the Holy Spirit, and they ask if this will be the arrival of a political renaissance for Israel. We, from hindsight, are aware of God's plan in empowering the Church to carry on His work, bearing witness to the world about Jesus' death, resurrection, and ascension. The disciples, however, were not so well informed. For three years they knew His unique companionship. The thought of carrying on God's work without His bodily presence may not have seriously entered their minds.

Why do the disciples think the political restoration of Israel is what Jesus is promising? For one thing, Jesus had spoken often about the coming Kingdom and had promised the disciples places of honor in the new order (Lk. 22:28-30). Also, the presence of God's Spirit had been associated in Jewish minds with the period of Israel's political sovereignty in the Old Testament. In the prophet Ezekiel's days, when Israel lost its sovereignty, the presence of God had been pictured as departing from Israel (Ezek. 10, 11).

1:7   Jesus' answer to the disciples' question is indirect, though it has negative connotations. He suggests that the timing of Israel's restoration is God's prerogative, implying that God may not have chosen the present time.

1:8   What will happen when the Spirit arrives? The disciples will receive power; they will be witnesses to the world. The areas of the predicted witness represent gradually enlarging circles of ministry and are an outline of the areas Luke covers in Acts. Jerusalem, of course, is the city in which the witness begins. Judea is the part of Israel that includes Jerusalem. Samaria is the region immediately north of Judea. "The ends of the earth" includes the apostles' outreach to the Gentile world.

1:9, 10   Jesus' ascension is still celebrated as an important event in the Church calendar, commemorating Christ's exaltation to the right hand of God. Commentator F. F. Bruce points out that this was not the first time Jesus had vanished from His disciples (Lk. 24:31), but this disappearing ends a series of visitations of Christ from "that exalted and eternal world to which His 'body of glory' now belonged." Jesus leaves in majestic style. A cloud, often a symbol of God's divine power and presence in the Old Testament and in the Gospels, hides Him from the disciples' sight. Perhaps they continue to gaze into space, hoping their Lord will reappear.

1:11   In this context the soft rebuke by the two men dressed in white is appropriate. They ask why the disciples are still standing around. Their promise confirms what Jesus Himself had said: that one day "all the nations of the earth . . . will see the Son of Man coming on the clouds of the sky" (Mt. 24:30). Although the two men are not identified, Luke's reference to their wearing white hints that they are angels.

1:12   The disciples travel back to Jerusalem from the Mount of Olives, which is the same place Jesus had gone the night of His betrayal. The distance Luke calls "a Sabbath day's walk"—because it was the distance the religious code allowed Jews to travel on the Sabbath—is just over one-half mile.

1:13, 14   After arriving in Jerusalem, the core group stays in the upstairs room of a house, awaiting the arrival of the Holy Spirit. Why did Jesus make them wait? He, too, had waited once, praying and fasting in the desert before beginning His public ministry (Mt. 4:1, 2). The apostles spend their time praying and reviewing what Jesus had taught them. Soon they will experience the Holy Spirit's outpouring in a dramatic way.

1:15-17 Dealing with Judas's vacancy is a sad change of pace in contrast to the preceding description of Christ's ascension. Yet these verses show the disciples' great respect for the authority of Scripture and its Lord. Donald Guthrie writes in *The Apostles,* "The most probable reason why the apostles wanted to keep the complement of twelve was because of the importance which the authority of Jesus had given to it." Peter, the recipient of Christ's great prediction about the Church (Mt. 16:18), and who, unlike Judas, accepts the Lord's forgiveness (Jn. 21:15-19), leads the discussion.

1:18, 19 These verses are in parentheses, indicating they were not part of Peter's speech but given as background information for Theophilus. Although Luke says Judas bought the field, Matthew 27:7 explains more specifically that the Pharisees purchased the field with Judas's money and most likely put it in his name. Judas's suicide not only brought disgrace to himself, but also made the field suitable only as a place to bury foreigners.

1:20 In verse 16 Peter reminds his listeners that David, in writing his Psalms, is a mouthpiece for the Holy Spirit. Now he quotes from Psalms 69:25 and 109:8, applying them to Judas. Because David is recognized as a type of the Messiah, his enemies can be regarded as typical of the enemies of Jesus. This principle makes the Scripture applicable to the apostles' situation.

1:21-23 The criteria for apostleship are that the candidates have followed Jesus from His baptism to His ascension, and that they have been witnesses of the resurrection. This suggests that sticking close to Jesus provides the best credentials. Those who qualify are Joseph (whose surname, Barsabbas, means "son of the sabbath" and who, like many Jews at the time, had a Gentile name: Justus), and Matthias, meaning "gift of Jehovah."

1:24, 25 For decision making, casting lots had precedent in Jewish history (Prov. 16:33), but the practice receives no other support in the New Testament. The believers' simple but trusting prayer translates effectively from the Greek: to the One who is "heart knowing."

1:26 Although not mentioned again in Scripture, Matthias, according to some church traditions, was one of the 70 disciples in Luke 10:1, and was a missionary in Ethiopia.

2:1 At its very beginning, the Church was not a collection of spiritual Lone Rangers. The disciples assembled together "with one accord" (KJV). Our faith, of course, has a strictly personal element—a relationship between a believer and God alone. But it also has a corporate dimension. Neither can be neglected without great loss. (See Hebrews 10:24, 25; I Corinthians 1:10; and John 17:23, which emphasize the need for fellowship.)

2:2, 3 Wind is an image Jesus uses to describe the Spirit (Jn. 3:8), and it plays a powerful role in resurrecting Ezekiel's dry bones (Ezek. 37). Here, it definitely is no harmless breeze.

Something like "tongues of fire" comes to rest on each of them. This may be difficult to picture, but remember, fire burns away impurities; so does the Spirit. Fire brings both heat and light; so does the Spirit. John the Baptist, prophesying the coming of the Christ, said, "He will baptize you with the Holy Spirit *and with fire*" (Mt. 3:11). What more appropriate sign could God use to introduce the Spirit's coming?

2:4 Two important phrases stand out in this verse. "Filled with the Holy Spirit," for the Jerusalem believers, meant the beginning of the Spirit's permanent availability and controlling influence. This they experienced in the baptism of the Spirit that marked Pentecost. Prior to this event, some of God's people experienced the Holy Spirit under special circumstances—the Spirit "came upon them." But now the Spirit's filling would be available to all believers (I Cor. 3:16; Eph. 5:18).

From this text it is important to realize that our access

to the Holy Spirit is immediate, depending on our willingness to allow Him to work.

The second phrase, they "began to speak in other tongues," is regrettably a subject of theological controversy. In the present context, the disciples receive this gift in order to address the gathered foreigners in languages they would understand. The purpose was to spread the Gospel. This *glossolalia* may have been different from the kind practiced by the Corinthian church, for Paul writes that tongue speaking could not be understood by others without an interpreter (I Cor. 14).

2:5-11 The "God-fearing Jews," who geographically and culturally come from many backgrounds, are in Jerusalem so they can attend special Temple convocations (Num. 28:26). The areas mentioned include present-day Turkey, Egypt, parts of Africa, and Italy.

2:12, 13 Here exists an example in which some religious-minded people are open to God's presence while others rationalize it away with something as foolish as 9 a.m. drunkenness.

For Discussion

1. What picture comes to your mind when you envision a "Spirit-filled" Christian? In what ways would you prefer to change this picture?

2. Can you name any instances in which you felt led, or empowered, by the Spirit? Describe the experience.

3. Is the concept of Spirit filling open to abuse? How?

2

What Do I Say?

Truth to Apply: I can find courage to witness as the Holy Spirit empowers me.

Key Verse: God has raised this Jesus to life, and we are all witnesses of the fact (Acts 2:32).

The word "witnessing" often exposes a neglected area in our lives and makes us feel guilty. Many Christians suffer paralysis of the mouth when it comes to sharing Christ with family and friends. Maybe you pray that your Christian walk, without any words, will be sufficient.

Yet Jesus clearly calls us to be verbal witnesses (Mt. 23:34-37). Our neighbor cannot know the source of our love without explanation. Goethe once said, "Nothing is more terrible than energetic ignorance." So, too, Christian zeal can be both aimless and arrogant unless it clearly shows its beginning and ending in Jesus Christ. This requires speaking the Good News.

Physical birth never produces instant maturity. A baby is nurtured for years, learning to walk and run, passing through several stages of development until maturity. Is spiritual birth the same? In what ways are the two similar? Different? If one of our "developmental tasks" is to learn to speak boldly for Christ, how should we view our first stumbling efforts?

Background/Overview: *Acts 2:14-47*

The New Testament word "witness," which is always a translation of the Greek word *martus* or one of its cognates, usually has a much broader meaning than modern Christians give it. It derives its primary force from its legal implications. H. Strathmann, writing in the *Theological Dictionary of the New Testament,* notes that "the proper sphere of *martus* is legal, where it denotes one who can and does speak from personal experience about actions in which he took part and which happened to him, or about persons and relations known to him." Witnessing is more than sharing a belief.

The word is often extended beyond the basic legal sense (without losing some flavor of the legal usage) to refer to the proclamation of truths of which the speaker is convinced. These two uses of the word are approximately equivalent to the meaning of the English expression "to bear witness." ("To bear witness" is the KJV translation for the verb form of *martus*.)

Light on the Text

2:14, 15

In Dallas, Texas, a Christian tourist attraction features a life-sized painting called "Miracle at Pentecost." This art depicts some 100 New Testament believers with whom Jesus interacted. A focal light rests on Peter, frozen in a running motion with his face excited and intense, his mouth open to proclaim the Gospel.

Standing with the eleven in the Temple's spacious outer court, a transformed Peter becomes God's mouthpiece. He begins by quieting the amazed onlookers with an explanation concerning the feeble accusation that they are drunk.

2:16-18

Here is the declaration that the prophecy in Joel 2:28-32 is coming true before them. The "last days" includes the span of time between Christ's ascension and His Second Coming.

2:19, 20 "The wonders and signs to be revealed in the world of nature . . . may have more relevance in the present context than is sometimes realized: it was little more than seven weeks since the people in Jerusalem had indeed seen the sun turned into darkness, during the early afternoon of the day of our Lord's crucifixion. And on the same afternoon the Paschal full moon may well have appeared blood-red in the sky in consequence of that preternatural event. These were to be understood as tokens of the advent of the day of the Lord" (F. F. Bruce, *Acts*).

2:21 Isn't it miraculous how the Gospel can be as simple to explain as this verse, and yet so involved as to require our whole life's study? The word "call" is the root behind the Greek word, *ekklesia,* which means a called-out assembly, and which our New Testament translates "church." This verse emphasizes the human side of the redemption process: we call on the Lord. Verse 39 stresses God's action in salvation: He calls to us.

2:22-24 Maybe you've heard of the Greek word *kerygma* [kuh-RIG-muh]. It stands for "preaching" and represents the elements of the Gospel the early church considered essential to pass on. Notice the kerygma Peter declares about Jesus. For example, he points out His humanity in verse 22: One from Nazareth, One approved of God, and One who lived among them.

2:25-35 Peter does an adequate job of explicating David's prophecy from Psalms 16:8-11 and 110:1. His statements carry a royal flavor: using *King* David, emphasizing God's sovereignty, and pointing to the King of Kings who resides on a heavenly throne. David's prophecy about Christ's resurrection, written so many years before His birth, can encourage us, who also must face the grave.

2:36 Peter's concluding words show his high view of Christ—the result of his three years of close association with the Master. Peter later again unites the terms "Lord," meaning God, and "Christ," meaning Messiah, in telling his audience to "sanctify in your hearts Christ as Lord" (I Pet. 3:15, ASV). These Jewish ears would be extremely sensitized to equating their divine title of "Lord" with Jesus. Yet Peter's declaration soon becomes a cheering slogan for the early Christians: "Jesus is Lord," Jesus is God (Rom. 10:9; I Cor. 12:3; Phil. 2:11). For the phrase "all Israel," compare Ezekiel 37:11.

2:37   Many in the crowd may have been among those who, just a few weeks before, had clamored for Jesus' death. Now Peter's words sting them, moving them to ask how they can set things right.

2:38   Peter's instructions are encouraging, hinting at the beautiful repentance and mercy passage of Joel 2:12, 13. Peter's audience would be familiar with John the Baptist's use of baptism as an external indication of the internal desire to repent. Baptism in Jesus' name enriches the ritual with its symbolism of death and resurrection. Its use was commanded by the Lord to identify those who are called by God.

Peter follows the two commands with a wonderful promise: believers will receive the gift of the Holy Spirit. The Greek word is *dorea*, "special gift," not *charisma*, "gifts," as in I Corinthians 12:4, 9, 28. Luke also refers to *dorea* in Acts 8:20; 10:45; 11:17.

2:39, 40   At the time, Peter might not have known the extent to which the Gospel would be given to Gentiles as well as Jews, but Luke, in hindsight, sees the prophetic significance. Peter is aware that his audience comes from a generation Jesus called faithless and corrupt (Lk. 9:41).

2:41, 42   Some 3,000 people turn to Christ as the result of Peter's bold, Spirit-directed preaching. Results come not from learning or eloquence, but as the Spirit's power works. The soundness of these conversions is shown by the fact that the converts are baptized, uphold the sound doctrine the apostles have received from Christ, and take part in the life of the church. Such are the marks of real Christians even today.

A little boy was accustomed to attending a church that had beautiful, stained-glass windows in the sanctuary. He was familiar with the Good Shepherd window as well as others that portrayed various events in the earthly life of Christ. Also in the church were windows with the figures of Saint Matthew, Saint Mark, Saint Luke, Saint John, and Saint Paul. These beautiful windows were a source of curiosity as well as impressiveness to the boy. One day as he was standing looking at them, an older member of the congregation approached him, and, pointing to one of the "saint" windows, asked, "What is a saint?" For a moment the boy seemed stumped for an answer, then, brightening up, answered, "A saint is a person the light shines through" (Earl C. Willer, *A Treasury of Inspirational Illustrations;* Baker Books).

2:42-47 Here are listed key activities the early church emphasized in its close-knit community life: studying God's Word, gathering together, observing the Lord's Supper, praying. Any church could begin on the path to spiritual renewal by studying and applying this text, and praying for the results of such "body life."

For Discussion

1. Share your experience with witnessing. In what ways have you been "successful"? How would you like to improve?

2. Where do you draw the line between boldness in witnessing and respecting the right of others to hold their own views about God and religion? Can one be too pushy?

3. What is the "starting point" in presenting the Gospel message to people in our day? What things do they need to see and hear from us in order to be drawn to Christ?

4. Is there validity in a witnessing approach that merely tries to get people to begin asking themselves the "right" questions about life's meaning? Explain.

3

Helping Hands

Truth to Apply: When I do acts of kindness in Jesus'
name, I am being used by the Spirit for a compelling
Christian witness.

Key Verse: Silver or gold I do not have, but what I
have I give you (Acts 3:6a).

One of the greatest opportunities for Christians to do
good works today is by extending mercy to the needy. A
cartoon showed an opulent pastor evangelizing a starving
child, and the words of the child were, "In Heaven will
there be enough food to eat?" Like the beggar by the
gate in Jerusalem, today's destitute and starving people
are looking for someone who will help them.

Gandhi never tired of repeating that there are enough
goods in the world for everyone's *need,* but not for
everyone's *greed.* Do you agree? In what practical ways
could you or your group help remedy some of the
inequities in your own community?

From Genesis to Revelation, in every stage of God's working, there is an *act* of God and a corresponding *revelation*. As in a well-wrought symphony, there are variations on the theme, but again and again the basic pattern emerges: there is a work and a word, an act and an acclamation.

For example, when Moses met with Aaron about the work of leading the people of Israel out of Egypt, "Moses told Aaron everything the Lord had sent him to say, and also about all the miraculous signs he had commanded him to perform" (Ex. 4:28). Also, in the burning bush Moses *saw* the fire and *heard* a voice.

Most importantly, the work/word theme became prominent in the ministry of Jesus. "He traveled throughout Galilee, *preaching* in their synagogues and *driving out* demons" (Mk. 1:39). Recall, too, the question John the Baptist's disciples asked of Jesus: "Are you the one who was to come, or should we expect someone else?" Jesus' answer? "Go back and report to John what you have *seen* and *heard*: The blind receive sight, the lame walk, those who have leprosy are cured, the deaf hear, the dead are raised, the good news is preached to the poor" (Lk. 7:20, 22).

So the Biblical background to Peter's miracle and message recorded in Acts 3 and 4 is wonderfully illuminating. This combination of work and word is God's usual way of operation! He works, then speaks. He refuses to work when He will not be listened to. And His work is not only through miracles, but through natural events and adversities.

Light on the Text

3:1 Luke probably chose to highlight this miracle because it was well-known. After all, the event marks the spiritual birthday of hundreds of Christians (Acts 4:4). Although John says nothing in the story, he probably is mentioned because Luke has a penchant for duality. We'll even see in Acts 12 that Peter is guarded by two soldiers and bound with two chains. More importantly, Jesus commands His disciples to go in twos (Lk. 10:1).

Because Jews reckoned the hours of the day from sunrise (rather than midnight), the ninth hour is about 3 p.m. The second daily Temple sacrifice was performed then.

3:2   Luke stresses that the man is lame from birth. The writers of the Gospels and Acts frequently accent the seriousness of the disabilities which God heals. They want us to know the healings are not merely the effects of psychological changes, but are truly miraculous transformations.

There is controversy over which gate was called "Beautiful," but many scholars say it was a gate leading from the outer court of the Temple (the Court of the Gentiles) into the Court of the Women, where the treasury was. Josephus, a first-century Jewish historian, says this gate was of Corinthian bronze and "far exceeding in value those plated with silver and set in gold." It could be that when Peter says, "Silver or gold I do not have," he points to this gate.

3:3-7   Luke the physician gives us a wonderful and vivid account of this man's healing. The nineteenth-century scholar Adolf Harnack writes, "That which the physician observes during the months of the ordinary gradual cure of a lame man is here compressed into a moment." There are three concrete, physical events: first, Peter and John look directly at the lame man and he returns their attention; the use of the name of Jesus Christ brings healing power; Peter touches him. In the Gospels, healings are performed in the name of Jesus, even the ones done by those who are not real disciples. Yet the name is not magical. Certain Jewish exorcists used the name of Jesus to cast out evil spirits, but they were powerless to perform any good, working themselves considerable harm (Acts 19:13-16).

3:8   The behavior of the man after he is healed bears striking resemblance to Isaiah's description of what will happen when the Messianic reign comes to pass (Isa. 35:6).

3:9, 10   The man's joyful reaction gathers a crowd, giving Peter a chance to proclaim Christ to them.

3:11, 12   Solomon's Porch, or Colonnade, was a long portico running the length of the east side of the outer court. A year before, Jesus had ministered there (Jn. 10:23), and in the years after Pentecost, it became a frequent meeting place for the Jerusalem Christians (Acts 5:12).

3:13-16   Observe the titles ascribed to Jesus.
     One can overlook the exemplary faith of the lame man, but Peter doesn't. As he clings to Peter and John, Peter mentions that although Christ has healed this man, it has occurred because of his faith.

3:17-20   Although Jesus' sufferings belong under God's sovereign plan, Peter does not mince words in placing the blame—ignorant though it was—on his listeners. In our culture, guilt, blame, and sin are ugly words we shy away from. But if we refuse to acknowledge our sin and repent, we also shut out the "times of refreshing" the Lord has to offer. He demands holy people.

3:21-26   One could do an edifying Bible study on how each Old Testament prophet forecasts the coming of Christ. Peter's sermon, like many of the speeches recorded in Acts, sadly explains that the Jewish people, heirs of the covenant, rejected their Messiah. Despite this, a remnant believes, and all peoples on earth who believe inherit the blessing (Rom. 11:11).

4:1-3   Observe carefully Luke's explanation for the opposition: "They were . . . teaching the people and proclaiming in Jesus the resurrection of the dead" (vs. 2). Throughout Acts, Luke stresses that the real offense is not so much political or moral, as it is doctrinal. The Church proclaims the resurrection of Jesus Christ. (See Acts 23:6; 24:15, 20, 21; 26:8.)

4:4   Luke, as a historian, frequently notes the numerical growth of the early church. Although these early chapters focus on Peter, one should remember how extremely busy (in the tasks of witnessing and nurturing) every disciple would be at this time. The joy and love in the early church must have been very attractive.

4:5-7 The Sanhedrin must have had an enormous headache over Jesus and His followers. When would it end? This supreme court of the Jews consisted of 70 leaders and the high priest. Annas, high priest from A.D. 6 or 7 to about A.D. 15, plus his five sons, and son-in-law Caiaphas, are the controlling power. Nothing certain about John and Alexander is known apart from this incident.

4:8-10 Who really stands on trial in this dialogue? Peter, filled with the Holy Spirit, defends himself with four points: the healing does no harm; it is accomplished in the name of Jesus, and in the evidence of His resurrection power; God has outwitted the religious leaders by raising Christ from the dead; Jesus is Lord and Savior, and salvation comes exclusively from Him.

4:11, 12 The idea of the Messiah as a rejected/exalted cornerstone appears in Psalm 118:22. Jesus refers to it in Mark 12:10, and during His passion He uses it to condemn those who plot His execution (Mt. 21:45). In *The Old Testament in the New Testament*, R. V. G. Tasker observes that this Old Testament verse about Jesus is "one of the passages most frequently quoted by the early Christian teachers to describe the temporary humiliation and subsequent rejection of Jesus the crucified and risen Messiah. . . ." (See Romans 9:33; Ephesians 2:20; and I Peter 2:6, 7.)

Verse 12 may make the secular humanist (or religious syncretist) wince. It declares that our witnessing must exalt Christ as the sole mediator between God and humanity.

4:13 Members of the the Sanhedrin (controlled by the pragmatic Sadducees, who rejected any resurrection belief) are startled by the dramatic change in Peter and John. They seem to analyze everything about the situation except the Gospel's message, which might pierce their hearts.

4:14-18 Some Jewish scholars believe the Sanhedrin could have squelched the Christian movement if it would have dealt more severely with Peter and John. However, the rulers could not deny the miracle; they could not produce the body of Jesus; they dared not displease a dazzled crowd.

4:19-22 An orthodox Jew would have second thoughts about disobeying his religious leaders, but Peter and John stand out like gems of courage. They cannot censor what is true and what they have experienced.

In *What's Gone Wrong with the Harvest* (Zondervan), James F. Engel and H. Wilbert Norton discuss why so many Christians find it difficult to communicate the Gospel. The authors suggest there is little or no harvest because the harvesting equipment of the Church has lost its cutting blades:

(1) A conviction that Jesus is Lord, even over the grave. A Christian who is convinced that Easter is a reality, and can defend this position, will exude confidence before the world.

(2) A conviction that Christ is able to change the lives of people today. If we see transformed lives on a regular basis, we will not doubt what the risen Christ can do.

(3) Filling with the Holy Spirit. His power is the dynamic for all Christian service.

For Discussion

1. What are the greatest needs of the people who live in the community surrounding your church?

2. What are some practical ways you, as an individual, could begin helping to meet some of these needs?

3. How could your church group begin having some impact on these problems?

4

Share, and Share Alike!

Truth to Apply: As a Christian, I am called to a fellowship marked by open hearts and shared possessions.

Key Verse: All the believers were one in heart and mind. No one claimed that any of his possessions was his own, but they shared everything they had (Acts 4:32).

Human life has two poles: the individual and the group. One of the functions of the Church since the earliest days of its existence has been to help individuals find themselves by incorporating them into the life of the Christian community. The local church must be a community in which persons can live together cooperatively and creatively.

In light of our natural tendency to focus on self-interests, we must really work at becoming a community in which private enterprise will be redeemed by a concern for public benefit. The right of private property is to many of us a necessary and natural stimulation to individual initiative. But where private enterprise exploits the life and talents of persons, where it monopolizes the fruits of the earth rather than sharing them with all humankind, it must be checked. The incentive for such self-imposed discipline is to be found where the first Christians found it: in Jesus. The power to practice that discipline is the power of the living Christ.

Someone has said that if Christianity wants to exert an influence on this chaotic world, it will not have its full effect through unrelated, though well-meaning, individuals. It will do it by being a community dedicated to a divine commission. Do you agree or disagree? Why?

Jesus had prepared the way for the climate of sacrificial sharing to flourish in the early church. Many of His teachings illustrated the dangers of focusing attention on position and wealth. As He taught about the camel and the needle's eye, the Lord concluded, "How hard it is for the rich to enter the kingdom of God!" (Mk. 10:23).

The common relief fund of the new church had been started right after Pentecost (Acts 2:41-47), when those who believed sold their possessions and pooled them for the good of all. The Christians found joy in worshiping together in the Temple and conducting Communion services in homes, sharing their meals with thankfulness and praise to God.

The infant church experienced God's blessings in the form of miracles (Acts 3:1-10) and preached in the power of the Holy Spirit (Acts 3:11-26). Its members were also feeling the beginnings of persecution for their faith and the premonition of more suffering to come. Peter and John were warned by the priests and scribes "not to speak or teach at all in the name of Jesus" (Acts 4:18). Their response: a firm declaration of their commitment to continue witnessing for the risen Christ.

These events form the immediate context of Acts 4:32-35. The climate of shared possessions, unity of spirit, and concern for the needs of others was the Christians' direct response to God's work in their lives.

Light on the Text

4:23   When the highest court of the Jews commands Peter and John to stop preaching, their response is, "We cannot help speaking about what we have seen and heard" (v. 20). Notice their next step: they seek out the support of the church, which in unison approaches God for help.

4:24-30 These verses contain a good model for praying done with the Old Testament finesse found in such passages as II Kings 19:15-19 and Nehemiah 9:5-37. The believers begin with praise to God and confidence in His sovereignty. They use Scripture, Psalm 2:1, 2, as part of their petition. This Messianic prophecy, declaring the mutual conspiracy of Jews, Gentiles, and earthly kings against Christ, is something they have witnessed.

4:27, 28   They express confidence that God's plan cannot be thwarted by such enemies. The noun "servant," used by the believers to describe Jesus and themselves, validates what they request. They do not desire safety, comforts, or even the grace to do more eloquent, less offensive witnessing. Rather, they ask for boldness and miracles which will glorify Christ.

4:31   Throughout Acts God's participation with His people is vibrant. He not only immediately answers their prayer, but shakes the meeting place, perhaps as a loving gesture of power to encourage them in facing future raging adversaries.

4:32   Although similar to 2:43-47, this passage emphasizes the spirit of generosity by introducing the contrast between Barnabas and Ananias and Sapphira. There is a clear implication: though the right of possession is not abolished, the needs of the community take precedent. Believers possess as though they possess not.

    The 19th-century preacher Charles H. Spurgeon observes, "The believers in Acts were not communists; they were Christians; and the difference between a communist and a Christian is this—a communist says, 'All yours is mine,' while a Christian says, 'All mine is yours'; and this is a very different thing."

4:33   "Grace" includes the idea of "the divine power which equips a . . . [person] to live a moral life" (*New Bible Dictionary*). Without it we cannot consistently put others above ourselves. It is a quality of life that becomes more evident the more it is exercised.

4:34, 35   The act of selling is the owners'; so is the act of handing the proceeds to the apostles. The community has nothing to do with the money until it is given. The distribution itself is determined by the principle of need, so that none lack.

4:36, 37	The few verses in Acts referring to Barnabas offer insight into a Spirit-filled Christian life—a life worth imitating. He demonstrates generosity and sacrifice, broad-mindedness (9:26, 27), a life filled with the Holy Spirit (11:24), a gift for preaching (11:23), trustworthiness (11:29, 30), and an adaptation to missionary work (13:2).
5:1, 2	Possibly Barnabas's example spurs Ananias and Sapphira to good intentions—which then slip into temptation and sin.
5:3, 4	Peter's question brings out the source of Ananias's sin: "How is it that Satan has so filled your heart that you have lied to the Holy Spirit . . . ?" Ananias's motives are not revealed, nor is the amount he keeps back. Peter's stern words focus directly on the terrible significance of his sin: it is a lie, and a lie to God. Ananias yields to the whispered temptation of Satan, making a mockery of the spirit of giving.
5:5, 6	Ananias does not die at Peter's hand. The expression "when Ananias heard this" suggests he recognizes Peter's stern judgment as the judgment of God. Probably the shame and guilt agitate him so strikingly that he falls down and dies (see Prov. 28:13, 14, 18). Burial on the same day of death was a common practice, although it does not explain why Sapphira is uninvolved.
5:7	Sapphira may arrive because she has grown alarmed at her husband's delay, or because Peter has sent for her.
5:8-10	Peter's question is a merciful opportunity for Sapphira to separate herself from her husband's sin. Her glib lie indicates her determination to stick to the fraud.
5:11	F. F. Bruce observes that Luke is primarily interested in including the story of Ananias and Sapphira "to emphasize the reality of the Holy Spirit's indwelling

presence in the church, and the solemn practical implications of that fact" (see I Cor. 3:16, 17). Luke also refuses to idealize the unity of the Christian body, remarkable as it was. He uses the term "church," or *ekklesia*, here for the first of 23 times in Acts. (The expression "to the church" is missing from many Greek manuscripts in Acts 2:47.)

Although a disturbing incident, Ananias and Sapphira's story can teach us some important lessons about our attitude toward sin. Jerry Bridges, in *The Pursuit of Holiness* (Navpress), explains: "We often say 'God hates the sin but loves the sinner.' This is blessedly true, but too often we quickly rush over the first half of this statement to get to the second. We cannot escape the fact that God hates our sins . . . ."

5:12-16 Luke has just written about an incident involving Satan's meddlings among believers. Next he tells how Satan stirs up the Sanhedrin to frustrate the early church's growth. Our writer, however, wants to present a balanced picture of the Holy Spirit's upper hand in such spiritual warfare. He again mentions the miracles, the church's growth, the power to heal and cast out evil spirits. One can imagine the uproar in Jerusalem—country folk crowding the narrow streets with their sick loved ones in the hopes of having Peter's shadow fall on them. Donald Guthrie, in *The Apostles* (Zondervan), points out that "although the method smacks of superstition, it witnesses to the strong belief in the power of the apostles."

5:17, 18 When a church does good works, it should not be surprised to find opposition. "Our struggle is not against flesh and blood," says Ephesians 6:12. The members of the Sanhedrin, dominated by the Sadducees, who deny the spiritual realm (Acts 23:8), are infuriated that the apostles continue to preach about Jesus coming back from the grave. Politically, too, they are concerned.

The church is attracting enthusiastic followers in a region known for radical political movements. The Jewish leaders are well aware that any revolt in Palestine would be crushed by Rome and that, in such a case, the imperial government would turn them out of power. Although a number is not given, the text seems to indicate that all the apostles are jailed. From a human perspective, can you think of a more precarious situation for the early church to face?

5:19, 20   Guards and jail doors are no match for God. The apostles, released by His messenger, return to Solomon's Colonnade. Their message is described as "life." What does this term suggest? The Bible is stubborn in its insistence that people without God are "dead in your trangressions and sins" (Eph. 2:1).

Many men and women who do not profess Christ seem very much alive. Yet in the sphere of the Spirit, each may be blind to the beauty of Jesus, deaf to the voice of the Holy Spirit, and unresponsive to God. Commentator William Barclay, reflecting on the apostles' courage, marvels, "They never asked, 'Is this course of action safe?' They asked, 'Is this what God wants me to do?' and then they laid aside the calculations of safety and obeyed. They were supremely willing to venture for God."

5:21-24   The Sadducees now call together all the Jewish leaders in the Sanhedrin. One can imagine the rationalizing they do in trying to explain the apostles' escape. Their mind-set, which denies the existence of angels, keeps them from knowing truth. Their false presuppositions lead to false conclusions.

5:25, 26   When guards reach the apostles, God's men offer no resistance. Had they balked, they would have had the crowds on their side and a dangerous confrontation might have arisen.

Again we notice the courage displayed by the followers of Jesus in the face of hostility. They show perfect peace in the midst of harassment. Peter later instructs Christians to "Be ready at any time to give a quiet and reverent answer to any man who wants a reason for the hope that you have within you" (I Pet. 3:15, Phillips).

5:27, 28   The high priest gives the apostles a compliment when declaring "you have filled Jerusalem with your teaching." Although his office should stand for fairness, he uses it only to authorize censorship.

5:29-32 Peter insists obedience to God is more important. This stance often comes into a discussion on whether a Christian should ever disobey civil authorities. Pastor Donald Grey Barnhouse suggests that civil disobedience is necessary when preaching the Gospel is jeopardized, or when a Christian is commanded to do an unchristian act.

5:33-39 Although the Sadducees are the Sanhedrin's majority, the Pharisees have more popularity. Among these leaders is Gamaliel, a respected teacher of such zealous students as Saul of Tarsus (Acts 22:3). Gamaliel's advice sounds reasonable: if these rebels have God on their side, nothing can squelch their movement. More likely, he persuades, the enthusiasm for Jesus will fizzle as it did for Theudas and Judas the Galilean.

5:40-42 Although God protects the apostles from death, they are not insulated from flogging. Jesus had warned them that persecution would be part of their calling (Mt. 10:17; Luke 12:11; John 15:18). Acts is a blessed record of victory in conflict, but it also shows the cost of walking in the footsteps of our Master.

For Discussion

1. Why do you think God punished Ananias and Sapphira so severely?

2. How important is it to have church support for your individual witnessing situations? Why?

3. Which is more difficult for you to do: witness by word or by deed? Does this lesson offer any fresh ways to help you strengthen your walk and talk with the Lord? Share specific applications to everyday life.

5

Attracted or Distracted?

Truth to Apply: I need to beware of distractions that can keep me from seeing God at work in my daily life.

Key Verses: But Stephen, full of the Holy Spirit, looked up to heaven and saw the glory of God, and Jesus standing at the right hand of God (Acts 7:55).

When the crowds heard Philip and saw the miraculous signs he did, they all paid close attention to what he said (Acts 8:6).

They're called gestalt—those splotch-and-blob pictures. You look at them one way and they look like nothing. Then, when your vision shifts, they look like something entirely different. For years a tract has circulated among Christians, a photo of flowers that is also the face of Christ. Another popular gestalt is a plaque of odd lines that spell "Jesus." Sometimes it takes a long time to focus correctly and recognize these concealed images. Some people never do see them.

The Jewish people suffered from a wrong gestalt in their understanding of God's historic plan. They focused on the bits and pieces (laws, their Temple) instead of the complete picture (salvation in Christ). Later, the early church also suffered from limited vision in understanding the full consequences of the Gospel for Gentile as well as Jew. Yet believers such as Philip and Paul did see the full picture sooner than other church leaders.

Our human frailties, too, result in each of us lacking God's total picture—"we see but a poor reflection." In what ways can Scripture be the spiritual glasses which correctly readjust our perspective on life?

Background/Overview: *Acts 6:1—8:40*

A large portion of this passage deals with two important New Testament personalities: Stephen and Philip. Stephen was one of the members of the early church selected by his peers to care for daily distributions to the poor. The people who served in this capacity were to be "known to be full of the Spirit and wisdom" (Acts 6:3). In addition to these required qualities, Stephen was "full of God's grace and power" (Acts 6:8). His ministry attracted widespread attention, and controversy swirled around him.

Stephen's teachings about the Gospel aroused the hostility of many Jews in Jerusalem, who initiated debates with him. Because Stephen's logic was irrefutable, his opponents hired informers to represent his arguments in the worst possible light (Acts 6:10-12).

The charge of blasphemy was brought against Stephen because of his remarks about the Law and the Temple. According to the false witnesses, Stephen taught "that this Jesus of Nazareth will destroy this place and change the customs Moses handed down to us" (Acts 6:14). Whatever Stephen said, it is clear that he not only quoted words spoken by Jesus, but interpreted their inner meaning. He likely understood that the Gospel meant the end of the ceremonial laws. He taught that the presence of God was not restricted to a single building or institution. And for these "heresies" he was brought to trial before the Sanhedrin.

Philip is the other person whose story is told here. The account of Philip's sensitive presentation of the Good News of Jesus Christ to someone from a different social, economic, racial, and national background is a central part of what can be called Luke's "ring theology." Jerusalem is the center ring. Each successive ring shows the spread of Christianity one step further away from Jerusalem until it finally arrives in Rome, the heart of the Roman Empire.

Luke gives us a layout of his ring theology in Acts 1:8. In that verse Jesus tells His disciples they will bear witness to Him "in Jerusalem, and in all Judea and Samaria, and to the ends of the earth."

Light on the Text

6:1-7 The early church wrestled with the problem of discrimination. The Aramaic-speaking Jewish widows of Palestine were getting more food than the Greek-speaking Jewish widows, who previously had lived in a Hellenistic culture. Instead of clinging to the enlarging bureaucratic responsibility of this task, the apostles wisely delegate the authority to other leaders "full of the Spirit and wisdom" (vs. 3). The entire congregation selects seven men, appropriately all with Grecian names.

Verse 7 mentions that the church is growing strong in leadership in other ways: "a large number of priests became obedient to the faith."

6:8-10 Apparently Stephen's work with food distribution does not hinder him from proclaiming Jesus in one of Jerusalem's synagogues frequented by Hellenist or Greek Jews. This man, "full of God's grace and power," delivers messages too convincing to counter.

6:11-15 Because they can't beat him in apologetics, jealous opponents trump up charges against Stephen, misrepresenting what he teaches. Stephen isn't so much against the Law and Temple as he is against their inadequacies in comparison to Christ. His listeners, however, depend on the Temple to draw crowds to their city, providing them with lucrative businesses. They use the "customs of Moses" to validate their life-styles.

7:1-8 Stephen's defense may strike the casual reader as a boring recitation of history, but he uses a popular Jewish device. The Jews saw history as the outworking of God's plan.

Eloquently, Stephen starts with history, as most of his accusers would have done in similar circumstances. But he gives it a different twist, showing how his accusers have violated the tradition they profess to defend. He states his case in the form of a review of God's dealings with the people.

Beginning with Abraham, Stephen argues that the presence of God is not restricted to any single land or building. He also mentions Abraham because Abraham heard God's summons and obeyed, venturing away from Ur to an unknown destination. Abraham's commitment was to God, not to some institution. He lived ready to move wherever God wanted him to.

7:9-16 The speech now moves to a second emphasis: the history of Israel is the story of Israel's rejection of God and the people He sends as their deliverers. The patriarchs, of whom the Jewish leaders boast, sold Joseph into slavery. But Joseph counted on God's presence and blessing, even in pagan Egypt.

7:17-43 Stephen mentions Moses as another deliverer who is rejected by those who should have welcomed his leadership. Again God acts, raising Moses to power and using him to set the people free. Stephen's point is that Israel rejects divinely appointed leaders throughout history, and in rejecting them, the nation rejects God.

7:44-50 Stephen next counters the charge that he has blasphemed the Temple. He reminds the Sanhedrin that the Tabernacle in the wilderness was not an ordinary structure but was divinely ordained. That beautiful tent, with its Holy of Holies, in which the cherubim looked down on the blood-sprinkled mercy seat, had been God's answer for the rebellious nation. Later, King David had initiated the erection of the Temple, which Solomon carried out. It had been intended to be an external symbol that would lead individuals to God. Instead, it became a consuming interest of Israel. Now individuals were neither the end nor the object of value, but they had become the means to an end. Their task was to keep the feasts, observe ceremonies, and support the Temple, thus continuing Judaism as an institution.

7:51 Having completed his logical defense of the Gospel, Stephen begins to attack his listeners, preaching to the people's conscience in the true spirit of God's prophet. (The suddenness of this attack leads some New Testament students to assume a heckler goads Stephen into this assault.) Stephen charges that the entire history of Israel is marked by resistance to the Holy Spirit.

7:52, 53

Not only the prophets had been rejected, but the One of whom the prophets spoke had been crucified. In Jesus' day the Jewish leaders paid homage to the slain prophets of an earlier age. They said, "If we had lived in the days of our forefathers, we would not have taken part with them in shedding the blood of the prophets" (Mt. 23:30). But the Master smashed their hypocrisy (Mt. 23:29-37). Stephen echoes that same charge in his defense.

7:54-60

What a contrast between the Spirit-filled Stephen and the enraged crowd. Because of all we know of this man's relationship with Christ we can understand more fully what Jesus means when He says that we gain life by losing it (Mt. 10:39).

Stephen's trial and death become a significant event in the life of the young Pharisee named Saul. As Augustine puts it, "The church owes Paul to the prayer of Stephen."

8:1-4

For Stephen, persecution occurs within a short span of time. For other believers suffering becomes a drawn-out ordeal.

Surely the believers fleeing Jerusalem could not have known how rapidly new churches would spring up throughout the world because of their faithful witnessing. The Good News spreads throughout Judea and Samaria. Stephen's death marks the beginning of the early church's reaching beyond Jerusalem.

8:5-8

Luke gives us the example of Philip, who first proclaimed the Gospel to the Samaritans. By orthodox Jewish standards the Samaritans were an outcast race. In 720 B.C. the Jews of Samaria (ten tribes of Israel) lost their racial purity because, when the conquering Assyrians brought other peoples into their land, the Samaria Jews eventually intermarried (II Kings 17:6-24).

This mingling of cultures created a new religious people. The Samaritans even had their own version of the Pentateuch and placed their temple on Mount Gerizim rather than Jerusalem. Now Philip, formerly an appointed caretaker in Jerusalem like Stephen, performs miracles among them and gains a responsive audience.

8:9-13, 18-24 Simon is an interesting character. Only God knows the depth of his belief. He is baptized, yet his heart is not right in God's sight. Power hungry, he depicts a person who can profess Christ and still be far from true inner commitment. An expert in sorcery, the man who had others following him (vs. 11) now dogs Philip (vs. 13), and later Peter and John (vs. 18), to discover the secret of obtaining the Holy Spirit (or, at least, the power to do miracles). His attempt to buy this special gift with money later inspires the word "simony."

Out of concern, Peter exhorts Simon and instructs him to pray to the Lord (vs. 22). Instead, Simon asks Peter to pray for him (vs. 24).

8:14-17, 25 When Peter and John journey to Samaria, they travel into unfamiliar territory. Though they had been in Samaria with Jesus prior to His resurrection, they had been forbidden to preach there (Mt. 10:5). John, along with his brother James, once had shown a condemning attitude toward a Samaritan village, asking for Heaven's fire to consume its inhabitants (Lk. 9:51-57). Now, after the Crucifixion and Pentecost, John prays for these Samaritans and lays his hands on them. The "Son of Thunder" indeed becomes the "Apostle of Love" as he and Peter witness throughout Samaria en route back to Jerusalem (vs. 25).

8:15-17 Why do you think God delayed giving the Holy Spirit to the Samaritans until the arrival of Peter and John? Bible scholar Charles C. Ryrie responds: "To answer this we must recall who the Samaritans were. They were half-caste Jews . . . who had their own rival worship system. 'The Jews have no dealings with the Samaritans' (Jn. 4:9). If the Spirit had been given to the Samaritans while Philip was preaching, then the Samaritans might well have thought that their brand of Christianity was distinct from the Judean brand just as their existing worship was distinct from Judaism. Thus there would have been two churches. But by the laying on of hands of Peter and John, apostles from Jerusalem, in the giving of the

Spirit, God assured unity in the infant church. The Samaritan movement was identified with that of Judea" (*The Acts of the Apostles,* Moody Press). In addition, the apostles could assure the Jerusalem Christians that God accepted Samaritans into His Kingdom.

8:26	Wouldn't you hesitate to follow the Spirit's leading if it seemed so peculiar? Philip's evangelizing is going wonderfully; then he is instructed to go to a desert road! But he immediately obeys.
8:27, 28	While God's Spirit works among the crowds, He never overlooks the single sojourner seeking Him. The Ethiopian eunuch, actually from present-day Sudan rather than present-day Ethiopia, has just completed a pilgrimage to Jerusalem. It has proven disappointing because his questions remain unanswered. He puzzles over Scripture.
8:29-35	Do you appreciate Philip's energy? He "runs" to the chariot. He asks a forward but disarming question. He explains Isaiah 53 as a Messianic prophecy fulfilled in Jesus. He also explains the need for repentance and baptism.
8:36-38	"Why shouldn't I be baptized?" is an important question in Luke's narrative. It speaks of the receptiveness of the Gentiles to the Gospel. The Holy Spirit has directed Philip to the man; he believes and is baptized (Gal. 4:26-29). His disappointment turns to joy.
8:39, 40	Philip continues preaching in many other towns until he reaches Caesarea. It appears he settles there. Twenty years later we find him with four Spirit-filled daughters (21:8, 9).

For Discussion

1. What qualities in Stephen and Philip do you find admirable? Think of the most impressive contemporary Christians you know. Are their priorities and qualities similar to those of Stephen's and Philip's?

2. Referring back to the definition of gestalt in the introduction, what kind of picture did the following people have of God: A. Sanhedrin   B. Stephen C. Simon   D. Ethiopian eunuch?

3. The Holy Spirit's power does not keep us from death, nor does it guarantee a comfortable life-style. What purposes does His power serve in our lives?

6

A New Start

Truth to Apply: God's transformation of unlikely candidates like Saul reminds me that the miracle of salvation is available to all—even those who presently resist the Gospel.

Key Verse: This man is my chosen instrument to carry my name before the Gentiles and their kings and before the people of Israel (Acts 9:15).

In one of the scenes of Shakespeare's _Hamlet_, the hero invites his mother, Queen Gertrude of Denmark, to see a play about a queen who says she loves the king so much she would never remarry. Hamlet asked his mother how she liked the play. Queen Gertrude, who Hamlet believes has murdered his father, replies, "The lady protests too much, methinks."

Is it possible that, like Saul, people today who are the most vocal in their opposition to Christianity are sometimes those who are in fact closest to conversion? Can you cite examples from your own experience?

Background/Overview: *Acts 9:1-31*

This lesson deals with the conversion of Paul. To become better acquainted with this servant of Christ, you may wish to study some pertinent biographical data (dates are approximate):

A.D. 1   Birth (for information on Paul's early life, consult Acts 21:39; 22:3, 28; II Cor. 11:22; Phil. 3:4-6).

33   Conversion (Acts 9, 22, 26).

33-36   Preparation for ministry in Arabian desert, and preaching in Damascus (Gal. 1:15-17).

36   Flight from Damascus and first visit to Jerusalem (Acts 9:20-29; Gal. 1:18-20).

36-45   Ministry in and around Tarsus (Acts 9:30; 11:25; Gal. 1:21).

45-46   Work in Antioch of Syria (Acts 11:26).

46   Second visit to Jerusalem (Acts 11:27-30).

47-49   First missionary journey (Acts 12:24—14:26). Probably after returning from this journey, Paul wrote Galatians to deal with the Judaizers.

49 or 50   Council at Jerusalem (Acts 15:3-35).

50-53   Second missionary journey (Acts 15:36—18:27). I and II Thessalonians written on this tour.

53-57   Third missionary journey (Acts 18:23—21:17). Letters composed on this journey: I and II Corinthians, Romans.

57   Arrest in Jerusalem (Acts 21:18—23:32).

57-59   Imprisonment in Caesarea (Acts 23:33—26:32).

59-60   Journey to Rome (Acts 27:1—28:15).

60-62   House arrest in Rome (Acts 28:15-31). During this first imprisonment in Rome, Paul wrote Philemon, Colossians, Ephesians, Philippians.

62-66   Period of release. Paul may have traveled to Spain as well as revisiting churches in Asia and Macedonia, and working in Crete. Paul wrote I Timothy and Titus during this time.

66 Second imprisonment in Rome. II Timothy written.

67 or 68 Death by beheading.

Reared in a fine Jewish home (Acts 21:39; 22:3; II Cor. 11:22; Phil. 3:5), Saul received his education as a young man in Jerusalem under respected Gamaliel (Acts 5:34; 22:3). According to Judaism, this Pharisee was a "good" man, not indulging in excesses of the flesh, keeping the tenets of the Law (Acts 26:4, 5; Phil. 3:6). His interpretation of the Law's purpose, however, was his blind spot: he knew obedience to rules but was a stranger to the Author and Finisher of faith. Yet, through the power of God, his life and theology would be radically transformed.

Luke believes Saul's conversion is so important that he includes three accounts of it: Acts 9, as part of his introduction into how the Gospel spreads throughout the world; Acts 22, as part of Paul's last public speech in Jerusalem; and Acts 26, as part of Paul's defense before Agrippa and Festus. Commentator I. Howard Marshall says part of the reason for three accounts, whose variations are minimal, is due to Luke's literary style. Also, "Luke is not trying to give us an account of what happened in precise detail but rather the general nature and significance of the event."

F. F. Bruce, in *Paul—Apostle of the Heart Set Free* (Eerdmans), claims Paul's major contribution to the world has been his presentation of the Good News of our salvation through God's free grace: "The free grace of God which Paul proclaimed is free grace in more senses than one—free in the sense that it is sovereign and unfettered, free in the sense that it is held forth to men and women for their acceptance by faith alone, and free in the sense that it is the source and principle of their liberation from all kinds of inward and spiritual bondage, including the bondage of legalism and the bondage of moral anarchy." The man who comprehends and communicates this message so well does so after his life-changing encounter on a dusty road to Damascus at high noon (9:1, 2).

Light on the Text

9:1   The brilliant light recalls the glory that shone on Moses' face on Mt. Sinai (Ex. 34:29); the description of Christ when He was transfigured before Peter, James, and John (Mt. 17:2); and the reaction of John upon seeing Christ standing among His churches (Rev. 1:16, 17). Paul's experience must have inspired him later to write II Corinthians 4:6.

How appropriate that the Pharisee of Pharisees, who will minister soon to Gentiles, encounters God outside of Judea. This interaction later provides validation for his apostleship. He asks the Corinthian Church, "Am I not free? Am I not an apostle? Have I not seen Jesus our Lord?" (I Cor. 9:1).

Also, after enumerating the post resurrection appearances of Jesus, Paul remembers, "And last of all he appeared to me also, as to one abnormally born" (I Cor. 15:8).

9:4   This verse and Acts 22:7 report that Paul fell to the ground. Acts 26:14 states, "We all fell to the ground." Can you give an explanation for the apparent discrepancy? Perhaps initially all fall to the ground, but Paul's companions rise while he remains prostrated until the Lord finishes His instructions.

9:5   "Lord" is used as a formal title much like the way we use the word "Sir." It is also God's title. In this verse and verse 4, Jesus indicates that to persecute one of His chosen is to persecute Him.

Acts 26:14 gives more information on the conversation between Jesus and Paul. The Lord addresses Paul in Hebrew, and concerning his persecution of believers He states: "It is hard for you to kick against the goads." A goad was an eight-foot wooden pole, with a spade at one end used for removing mud from the plow. The other end was a sharp point for prodding oxen. The intended meaning is that, like oxen futilely kicking against the goads, Paul uselessly resists a greater power (*The Zondervan Pictorial Bible Dictionary*).

9:6, 7 One can wrongly assume this conversation is quite brief. Acts 26:16-18 goes into more depth about the commission Jesus bestows on Paul to preach to Jew and Gentile and to be assured His protection is with him. Read verse 7 again with Acts 26:14 and Acts 22:9. Some commentators believe a discrepancy exists in the accounts concerning whether Paul's companions see and hear what he experiences. Put your thinking cap on before reading further, and determine how the passages complement one another. You might reason that all on the road experience something unusual: the companions see a light, they hear some kind of noise; Paul, however, sees The Light, hears The Voice. Their depth of perception probably varies.

9:8, 9 Without sight, food, or drink, Paul has time to consider what Christ is calling him to do. This high-energy, impatient person must sit and wait for God's next instructions.

9:10-14 Who remembers the persons who spiritually nurtured Martin Luther or Charles H. Spurgeon? Like such unknowns, Ananias is often that forgotten man on a Bible quiz, yet he has the distinction of being the man who helped Paul start his mission for Christ. A Jewish Christian, Damascus resident, and respected individual (22:12), Ananias has a relationship with the Lord that is fresh and candid. He asks for clarification in the vision he has concerning Paul: "Lord, am I understanding right? Did you say Saul the persecutor?" Once he's certain, Ananias makes his way for Straight Street. This Ananias, unlike the one in Acts 5, lives up to the meaning of his name, "God has been gracious."

9:15-18 In retrospect, the commission for Paul to preach to the Gentiles sounds glorious: salvation will reach the peoples of the world because of his influence. Yet in conversation with Christ and in reaffirmation through Ananias, Paul realizes that persecution awaits him. (Look up II Corinthians 11:23-30 for a list of Paul's sufferings and think about his example in light of Matthew 5:11, 12; Romans 8:17; II Timothy 2:11-13.)

9:19-22 This new life includes growth (being with the disciples) and witnessing. Although Paul's missionary work will not begin for at least three years, he cannot keep the Good News bottled up within himself. This is the only place in Acts where the title "Son of God" is used. C. I. Scofield explains, "Compare 2:36. Peter, while maintaining the Deity of Jesus ('God hath made that same Jesus, whom ye have crucified, both Lord and Christ'), gives special prominence to His messiahship. Paul, fresh from the vision of the glory, puts the emphasis on His deity. Peter's charge was that the Jews had crucified the Son of David (2:25-30); Paul's, that they had crucified the Lord of glory (I Cor. 2:8). In the KJV the sense is largely lost. The point was, not that the Christ was God . . . , but that Jesus, the crucified Nazarene, was the Christ and therefore God the Son."

9:23-25 Paul's on-target preaching does not change his listeners' hardened hearts. They are baffled and hateful. In II Corinthians 11:32 we find more detail on Paul's conflict with Damascus authorities. Damascus borders the "Arabia" Paul mentions, which was called the Nabatean Kingdom ruled by Aretas IV (9 B.C. to A.D. 40). Paul's witnessing in and around Damascus apparently irks the authorities, who determine to arrest him. God spares him with help from local believers.

9:26, 27 Some commentators place a three-year gap between verses 25 and 26. Paul spends three years in Arabia before going to Jerusalem (Gal. 1:17, 18). Even this time span does not convince the Jerusalem believers he is trustworthy. Barnabas serves as a successful mediator. Today's church also needs initiating "Barnabases" to bridge relationships among Christians in conflict.

Luke's reference to Paul's meeting with the "apostles" should be viewed as a "generalizing plural." F. F. Bruce explains that he does not visit all of them, only Peter, and James the brother of Jesus (whom he apparently regards as an apostle).

9:28-30 Having a common cultural background with the Grecian Jews, Paul gravitates toward them. He also may want to continue Stephen's work (which he was partially responsible for terminating).

The reception has not improved since Stephen's death. The "brothers" rescue him, sending him to the seaport town of Caesarea (where Philip perhaps offers assistance—8:40) and onward via ship to home base, Tarsus.

9:31 Luke's narrative of the early church's persecution and the conquering of Paul's heart ends with a respite. We might too casually pass over the meaning of a church body enjoying "a time of peace," since our church freedom is often assumed from Sunday to Sunday. Yet this gift from God deserves thanksgiving anytime. It must never be taken for granted.

As we mull over these verses concerning Paul's remarkable conversion, certain lessons about God stand out:

(1) Divine Love. The Savior cares about a man who persecutes Him and His followers. Christ seeks out Saul for the purpose of saving him. Paul himself knows he is the object of divine love. He writes that he was a blasphemer and persecutor, but "I was shown mercy" (I Tim. 1:12, 13). God loves sinners; that is the truth heralded in Saul's conversion story. It is a truth that offers assurance to all believers.

(2) Divine Intervention. Christians are supernaturalists. They know God is not restricted by the natural order. They believe He breaks into history. In the Biblical account of Saul's conversion, we see an outstanding example of divine intervention. Saul is bound for Damascus on a hateful mission, but Christ steps in. Here is the account of our conversions as well. You and I were bound for someplace, but Jesus found us—and now life is different! This lesson about divine intervention teaches hope. With God, impossible situations find solutions. Closed doors become gateways to new opportunities.

(3) Divine Power. The Savior transforms a hostile sinner, Saul; and if He can save a person like that, then Jesus can do something about those persons we are tempted to consider beyond redemption.

For Discussion

1. What can we do to develop concern for the eternal fate of loved ones?

2. Why are Christians sometimes pessimistic about whether family members will ever become Christians?

3. Paul is prepared to give his testimony on any occasion. Can you formulate a few sentences that summarize your first encounter with Christ? Share your own conversion experience.

7

No Favorites

Truth to Apply: Through the power of the Gospel, I can break down the barriers of prejudice in myself and in my church.

Key Verses: I now realize how true it is that God does not show favoritism but accepts men from every nation who fear him and do what is right (Acts 10:34, 35).

If you think you've conquered discrimination, try this exercise: form a mental picture of the saints gathered around Christ in Heaven.

Now be honest. Is the group an instant mix of red, brown, yellow, black, and white? Or is it just the group that happens to have your skin color, or that practices your way of worshiping the Lord?

Though the Jewish Christians had believed all their lives that segregation was God's plan, when God showed them something new they were open to it. Specifically, they accepted other races into full fellowship. Obviously, this means welcoming people into our own churches, regardless of their race or background. What attitudes enable us to receive a person of another race or culture into full fellowship?

We are first introduced to Cornelius in Acts 10. By profession, he is a centurion of the Roman army, with duties similar to those of a modern-day army captain. He is directly in charge of 100 men. In character, Cornelius is described as "devout and God-fearing" (Acts 10:2). He apparently believed in the God of Judaism and sought God's approval by adhering to the Jewish customs of giving and prayer.

Even so, the custom of the day was separatism. Jews did not ordinarily associate with or accept hospitality from Gentiles—a practice rooted in the traditions of the culture. A dietary custom forbade a Jew from eating food that had been declared ceremonially unclean. To do otherwise meant that the offender had to go through detailed purification.

Against this background and training, God selected Peter to break the mold and illustrate the New Covenant of acceptance through Jesus Christ.

In Acts 11, we see Peter under censure from Jewish Christians in Jerusalem because of a supposed violation of the Law. The offense: eating and associating with "unclean" Gentiles.

Light on the Text

9:32-35 Peter travels "about the country." Like any conscientious leader of God's people, Peter answers a cry for help. Aeneas has been bedridden for eight years with "palsy"—a malady due to paralytic stroke. Peter knows he has no special power in himself. Only Christ's power can heal validly. This miracle, like others recorded in Scripture, is important on two levels: first, it is the merciful healing of a sick man—God cares about individuals. Second, it is a dramatic witness to God's power, serving to "turn" many others to the Lord.

9:36-41 More populated today than in Peter's day, Tel Aviv served as Jerusalem's port. Resident Dorcas, whose name means gazelle (a symbol of beauty and grace) exemplifies God's love for one's neighbor. She was known for her good deeds and help of the poor.

Notice that the burial was delayed. The Christians of Joppa must have had faith that Peter could raise Dorcas.

9:42, 43 The results of Dorcas's miracle are the same as they were for Aeneas: people believe in the Lord (vss. 35, 42). Luke often shows an interest in names and occupations, particularly those who open their homes (Lk. 10:5-7; Rom. 12:13). Here Peter stays with Simon, whose profession would make his house unsuitable for the more scrupulous Jews.

10:1, 2 Caesarea, built between 25 and 13 B.C. by Herod the Great, was a magnificent city on the Mediterranean. It was the hub of caravan routes between Tyre and Egypt, and attracted quite a bit of sea trading. Palaces, public buildings, a huge temple and amphitheater enhanced its streets. The official residence of the Roman procurators, it also had a strong military presence, including the centurion Cornelius. Although paganism claimed many Caesareans, Cornelius is a "God-fearer," attracted to Israel's Yahweh (or Lord).

10:3-8 God promises that those who hunger and thirst for righteousness will be filled. Cornelius's longing for God, evident by his prayers and generosity, results in spiritual blessing.

The Greek word for "memorial" appears in Leviticus 2:2, where it is the part of the meal offered to God.

Just as some Christians are amazed when prayers receive immediate answers, Cornelius is startled by the angel who tells him how he can learn more about God. He immediately obeys, sending like-minded men under his authority to find Peter in Joppa, 30 miles away.

10:9-16 Notice God's perfect timing in these events. It was uncommon for Jews of that day to eat a noon meal. Rather, they ate lightly in midmorning and more substantially in late afternoon. Peter's hunger interrupts his praying, and he asks for food (which probably was ready when the three unexpected guests arrive).

What does this vision mean? Leviticus 11 spells out the Jewish food laws, prohibiting the eating of certain animals. Among four-footed beasts, for example, Jews could eat only those which both chewed cud and had cleft hooves, such as goats and cows. Pigs were off limits, considered "unclean," or unholy. Because Gentiles were often careless about specifics concerning these dietary laws, Jews refused to eat meat and other foods handled by them.

In Peter's vision the mixing of clean and unclean animals confuses him. He refuses to listen to the voice commanding him to eat. Yet three times Peter is told, "Do not call anything impure that God has made clean."

10:17-23   God teaches Peter in two ways: by allowing him to think out the vision's meaning; and by assuring him that it was right to go with Cornelius's men. The result is Peter's conclusion that what applies to food applies to people: "God has shown me that I should not call any man impure or unclean" (vs. 28).

10:24-29   When Peter arrives, Cornelius's house is full of people. The centurion unselfishly anticipates an experience he does not want others to miss.

Cornelius's bowing down to Peter may be simply out of respect, but Peter immediately reiterates to another what he has so recently, vividly, learned for himself—that God is certainly no respecter of persons: "I am only a man myself" (vs. 26).

10:30-33   Cornelius's comment in verse 33 that this group gathers "in the sight of God" (Revised Standard Version) is not overlooked by I. Howard Marshall: "This incidental remark indicates that when people gather together to hear the gospel . . . they do so in the presence of God. This appears to be the only use of this phrase in this sense in the New Testament, although the thought that men's actions are visible in God's sight is common."

10:34, 35   Peter proceeds to present the Gospel. F. F. Bruce says that because of the way the speech translates awkwardly in Greek and flows smoothly in Aramaic, Peter probably speaks in Aramaic and has a Greek interpreter.

The themes in Peter's message are the *kergyma* which the early church stresses (see the comments on 2:22-24). Fortunately for all believers, Peter explains, God does not pay attention to external appearances like color, position, rank, or popularity. What are God's qualifications for acceptance? Those who fear God and do what is acceptable to Him (vs. 35). The word "nation" in verse 35 is the Greek word *ethnos* which can also be translated "ethnic group." We can say that from every ethnic group God calls people to Himself.

10:36-43 The content of Peter's message is similar to others we have studied in Acts, particularly chapters 2 through 4. Refresh your concept of what the Gospel includes by picking out the key ideas Peter stresses about God the Father, Jesus, unbelievers, and believers.

In verse 43, Peter's reference to all the prophets, having insight into God's plan of salvation for the Gentiles may include Isaiah 53:4-6 and Jeremiah 31:34.

10:44-48 What occurs next interrupts Peter's speech and shocks his Jewish companions. The gift of the Holy Spirit, as on Pentecost, comes to Gentile believers! The reception is placed on the same level as what happened to the first disciples in chapter 2. The speaking in tongues and proclaiming of God's mighty works are further proof to Peter and his Jewish friends that God has done a work among Gentiles equal in impact to what He has been doing among the Jews. God shows no partiality. Peter remembers Jesus' words in Acts 1:5. These believers are baptized into the Church.

11:1-16 While Peter stays in Caesarea to teach, news of the unusual happenings among Gentiles travels back to Jerusalem. The Jewish Christians, like Peter in reaction to his vision, cannot understand what is going on. At this point they see their faith as a kind of reformed Judaism, still exclusive. They reason: "This is all wrong. If Gentiles want to come to The Way, they must come through the Mosaic Law and be circumcised. Did not Jesus also do this?" The more they think about what non-Jewish people in the church could mean, the more uncomfortable they become.

11:17 Peter emphasizes that it is God who directs the coming together of Jew and Gentile in faith. He admits a momentary misgiving in the situation, but his question assumes the right answer.

11:18 Unlike the Pharisees, who are so in love with their routine that they often miss what God is doing right in front of them, the Jewish believers see God's hand at work here. Their joyous response prepares them for expanding the Gospel's outreach to many Gentile households.

11:19-21 Antioch, with 500,000 people, was the third largest city in the Roman Empire. Located in Syria, it was the first place referred to in Acts where the Gospel moved beyond Judea, Samaria, and Galilee. The *Zondervan Pictorial Bible Dictionary* says, "Its citizens are a vigorous, aggressive race, famous for their commercial aptitude, their licentiousness, and the scurrility of their wit." F. F. Bruce adds that terms like *kyrios* ("Lord") and *soter* ("Savior") were popular to these pagans whose cults sought a divine lord to guarantee immortality.

11:22-24 The Jerusalem church wisely sends Barnabas, a Cypriot Jew (4:36; 9:27), to check out the Antioch stories. He's pleased with what he discovers. These verses are full of words and phrases depicting the many advantages of being a Christian. In Greek the word "encourage" means, like today, comfort and consolation, but it also includes confronting, admonishing, and teaching. Barnabas's duties encompass the total definition.

11:25, 26 The work becomes so great that Barnabas needs help in supervision. He travels to Tarsus to find Saul, who agrees to teach in Antioch.

The name "Christian" (adherent of Christ) is given to believers by pagans. " 'Christos'—the Greek form of the title Messiah—might be the name of an office to Greek-speaking Jews, but to the pagans of Antioch it is simply the name of a man of whom these people are always talking: a curious name, to be sure, unless it is the same as the common slave-name 'Chrestos' ('useful'). 'Who are these people?' one Antiochene would ask another, as two or three unofficial missionaries gather a knot of more or less interested hearers around them. 'These are the people who are always talking about Christos, the Christ-people, the Christians' " (Bruce).

11:27, 28   The prophetic gift in the early church, like that of tongues, was exercised under God's inspiration. It was, however, expressed in ordinary language. Agabus, who also may be the one in Acts 21:10, 11, foretells a severe famine.

For Discussion

1. In the Bible many people, like Aeneas and Dorcas, are healed, whereas most remain in their difficult circumstances. Isn't this favoritism, or discrimination?

2. Can you think of modern examples where racial or ethnic discrimination counters God's plan?

3. How can your church build bridges to those of a different ethnic group?

8

When Opposition Hits

Truth to Apply: Through study of the experience of the disciples, I can learn how to handle opposition to the work of spreading the Gospel.

Key Verse: "We must go through many hardships to enter the kingdom of God," they said (Acts 14:22b).

The apostle Paul insisted in one of his letters that what validated his authority to speak was the fact that, as far as the world was concerned, he was an imposter, dishonorable, unknown, dying, punished, poor, and negligible (II Cor. 6:8 ff.). To live the life of a committed Christian witness is obviously no guarantee of protection from all hardship. Jesus Himself said it this way: "In this world you will have trouble" (Jn. 16:33). How does this translate into your own life? Can you give any examples of opposition you have faced specifically because of your Christian faith?

Background/Overview: *Acts 12:1—14:28*

This passage offers insight into dealing with adversity, but it comes to us through observing God's people in the fighting ring. As you study you will want to discern how these examples can help you in what you have to overcome.

The four generations of Herods in the New Testament can be confusing. Herod the Great, puppet governor for the Romans, is tricked by the Wise Men and forces Joseph and Mary, with baby Jesus, to flee to Egypt (Mt. 2). After his death, three sons inherit his territory: (1) Archelaus, (2) Herod Antipas, and (3) Philip. Son Herod Antipas is called "that fox" by Jesus (Lk. 13:32), beheads John the Baptist (Matt. 14), and interrogates Jesus the night before the crucifixion (Lk. 23:7ff.). At the death of son Philip, Herod the Great's grandson, Herod Agrippa (fathered by Aristobulus), takes over Philip's reign. He eventually acquires the entire jurisdiction enjoyed by his grandfather. This is the boastful Herod we encounter in Acts 12. Later his children, Drusilla, Agrippa II, and Bernice show interest in the Gospel.

Light on the Text

12:1, 2   Although death and violence remain enemies of Christianity, they have been ultimately defeated by our resurrected Lord. James, the first martyred apostle, goes to Him who foreknew his death (Mk. 10:39).

12:3   The seven-day Feast of Unleavened Bread (Lev. 25:5-8) immediately follows Passover and becomes an appropriate time for Herod to seek loyalty from his Jewish subjects. Since James's death (and perhaps the deaths of others) has pleased the Jews, he seeks out the top ringleader of those following The Way.

12:4-11   Sixteen guards watch Peter in four-man shifts. Two protect the door; two are shackled to him.

Peter's easy escape, thanks to an angel, reads like a mystery thriller without the bloodshed. Supernatural elements make Peter think he is dreaming. Once the angel disappears and Peter is left in cold and darkness, he understands and declares God's protection.

12:12-17 Before going underground, he hurries to the home of Mary and her son John Mark, a young man who gradually becomes a key church worker over the next 30 years. Although the believers are praying for Peter, God surprises them with His answer. Peter leaves instruction to share information about his escape with James, the brother of Jesus, and others who probably form another house church in the city.

12:18, 19 "No small stir" is how the King James Version describes the Roman guards' commotion. On the day Herod plans to execute Peter he demands the lives of his guards instead. Other business takes Peter to Caesarea.

12:20 Caesarea lies north of Jerusalem and south of Tyre and Sidon. We do not know why these Phenician cities have displeased Herod, but they depend on his land (Galilee) for food. Blastus, Herod's chamberlain, gains their leaders an audience with the ruler; the meeting which turns into a public relations festival.

12:21, 22 The Jewish historian Josephus agrees with Luke's account, adding more description: ". . . Herod put on a robe made of silver throughout, of altogether wonderful weaving, and entered the theater at break of day. Then the silver shone and glittered wonderfully as the sun's first rays fell on it, and its resplendence inspired a sort of fear and trembling. . . . Immediately his flatterers called out from various directions. . . ."

12:23 The king's refusal to deny blasphemy is his downfall. Josephus records that when Agrippa accepts deification, he is struck suddenly by abdominal pain and dies five days later. Concerning Luke's account, I. Howard Marshall explains: "Eaten by worms can be taken quite literally . . . although it appears to have been a stock phrase in describing the death of tyrants. Appendicitis leading to peritonitis would fit the symptoms . . . and with the lack of medical hygiene in the ancient world roundworms could have added to the king's sufferings. W. Neil suggests a cyst produced by a tapeworm." Records show Agrippa died in A.D. 44 at age 54.

12:24 Use of the conjunction "but" indicates Luke does not view Agrippa's death as evening the score in losing James and forcing Peter underground. The gates of hell, however, cannot stop the church's encouraging growth.

12:25 This verse may seem out of place, but Luke is simply tying up the historical loose ends he has presented earlier. Whereas Agrippa dies in A.D. 44, a probable date for the famine-relief visit of Barnabas and Paul is A.D. 46. Having discharged the fund from the Antioch church to the Jerusalem Christians, Barnabas and Paul return to Antioch, taking John Mark with them.

13:1-3 The rest of Acts shows how the Gospel spreads throughout the Roman Empire, thanks to the tireless efforts of Paul and company, plus the support of this heterogeneous church.

Even from a few descriptive words, we can see that the Antioch church leaders are a mixed bag of cultures. Besides Paul, there are Barnabas, devout Jew from Cyprus; Simeon, called Niger (or "dark-complexioned one"); Lucius of Cyrene (a northern African city); and Manaen, reared in the royal court with Herod Antipas.

Despite differences, their unity in worship, prayer, and fasting allows them to discern God's will, and they send out their best teachers. Laying on of hands indicates a oneness in spirit and purpose.

13:4 Paul, Barnabas, and John Mark first travel 16 miles to Seleucia, the nearest seaport, where they catch a ship to the island of Cyprus, Barnabas's homeland.

13:5 Cyprus natives are influenced by the Greek goddess Aphrodite. Salamis is the island's major commercial city. Here, and consistently throughout Paul's ministry, he preaches first in the synagogues. This practice usually garners both a support group and jealous enemies.

13:6-12 The reception throughout Cyprus appears favorable, and Barnabas, with John Mark, returns later for follow-up (15:39). At Paphos, the island's capital, only one individual's opposition is recorded. This magician doesn't let up on the apostles' meeting with proconsul Sergius. Fearless confrontation is the appropriate response by Paul here. Bar-Jesus, like Paul on the road to Damascus, is temporarily blinded.

13:13 Sailing 175 miles to Attalia, Paul and Barnabas travel 12 miles inland to Perga. The lowland is hot and humid, with rampant malaria. They may be discouraged or at least inconvenienced by the loss of their helper, who heads for home.

Despite John Mark's immaturity in giving up, a valuable lesson can be learned from him: later, he does not allow this one mistake to hinder him from continuing on with the Lord.

13:14, 15 Paul and Barnabas climb the Taurus Mountains and reach the plateau beyond. Pisidian Antioch is a southern military stronghold for the Romans in what was called Galatia territory in Asia Minor. It is the setting for an important, lengthy message by Paul, given at the invitation of the local synagogue.

13:16-41 Paul's sermon compares to Peter's in Acts 2:14-36 in at least three ways: both ground their messages in Scripture (Isa. 55:11); each has one main theme—the Lord Jesus Christ; each emphasizes the Cross and Resurrection, which point to Jesus as the Messiah. When you read this sermon you may notice how Paul tries to include the God-fearing Gentile listeners (vss. 16, 26, 39, 40). These people often form the core of his newly planted churches.

13:42-45 The wonderful Gospel amazes this crowd. Here is another lesson about opposition: sometimes we wrongly presuppose the majority "out there" opposes the Gospel. Instead, many may be receptive to the message. For a week, Paul and Barnabas encourage eager listeners in small-group conversations. By the next Sabbath the town is buzzing about "the word of the Lord" (vs. 44).

13:46-50 Opposition comes from jealous Jewish leaders who use their influence to persuade civic leaders, both women and men, to expel the visitors. Notice how the disciples exhort the Jewish leaders for not considering themselves "worthy of eternal life" (vs. 46). The question is, what do these adversaries consider worthy? "This is the decisive moment in the development of the church. Up to this point the missionary efforts have been directed to the Jewish synagogue. Gentiles have come as proselytes through the influence of Jews who have become Christians. Now converts with no adherence to Judaism will spread the gospel in ever increasing geometric proportions" (*Community Bible Study Commentary*).

13:51, 52 In protest to expulsion, Paul and Barnabas do as Jesus commanded in Matthew 10:14. This symbolizes a release of responsibility. Paul, Barnabas, and the new believers exhibit qualities the authorities cannot take away.

14:1-5 Ninety miles east of Pisidian Antioch on the Roman highway is Iconium, an oasis between mountains and plains, with wheat fields and fruit trees. Many accept Christ and miracles occur. Again opposition begins with resistant Jews, who then ally with nonbelieving Gentiles.

14:6-10 Lystra has few Jews and no synagogue. Although the residents communicate with the disciples in Latin, they converse among themselves in Lycaonian.

Although many miracles occur on this first missionary venture (14:3), this is the only one Luke describes. Seeing some similarities to the healing by Peter in Acts 3, some critics suggest Luke manufactures this incident to give Paul as much stature as Peter. The differences do not fit into this theory. For example, this healing, unlike the one in Acts 3, has a horrendous effect.

14:11, 12 Paul and Barnabas may not know the local legend penned by the Roman poet Ovid, born a generation before Christ. He tells the story of an elderly couple unknowingly entertaining Zeus and Hermes. After the healing of the cripple, the Lycaonians take the dignified, muscular Barnabas for Zeus, and spokesman Paul as his herald, Hermes.

14:13 We cannot underestimate the hurdle Paul and Barnabas have to overcome here, so deeply ingrained is the religion of these simple people. Canon Michael Green observes, "Country religion of this sort resisted the Gospel to the last, and much of it survived (and still survives covered with a thin veneer of Christianity). The approach of Paul and Barnabas is to urge the reality of a single Creator God, who, so far from needing to be sustained by offerings, is himself the gift of all" (*Evangelism in the Early Church,* Eerdmans).

14:14 Tearing the clothing was a typical, dramatic way of registering horror at the utterance of blasphemy. It indicated one's complete disassociation from it (Mt. 26:65).

14:15-18 You may notice Paul does not utter Jesus' name or even use Scripture. His approach, however, is common for a Jewish apologist speaking to the unconverted. Although the "Old Testament Scriptures are not specifically called upon, they are not far beneath the surface. The whole approach is reminiscent of great passages in Isaiah and the Psalms where a stinging indictment of idolatry is delivered" (Michael Green). It would be pointless for Paul to preach Jesus as Lord if He were merely to be added to the already overcrowded lengthy list of gods. These people need to know the one true God, Jesus being the manifestation of Him.

14:19-21 Much in the style of a zealous persecuting Saul, Jews travel the 90 miles from Antioch and 20 miles from Iconium to snuff out the evangelists. A fickle mob stones Paul, who mentions this incident in II Corinthians 11:25. His recovery is miraculous.

14:22-25 They could have taken a different route to Antioch, Syria, but they retrace their journey to nurture the infant churches. Some scholars believe the Epistle to the Galatians is addressed later to these believers.

14:26-28 Almost a year from when they started, with 1500 miles under their sandals, Paul and Barnabas return to Antioch and share, not the good and bad from a human perspective, but "all that God had done through them and how he had opened the door of faith to the Gentiles."

For Discussion

1. Would today's Christian disciples have more boldness and perseverance if they had actually lived with Jesus physically, as the early disciples did? Do we have an unfair disadvantage because of our "distance" from the Jesus of history? Why or why not?

2. What is the most difficult opposition facing you right now? How is your Christian faith helping you in the midst of it? Do you see any parallels between your experience and that of the early disciples?

9

Culture Clash

Truth to Apply: I must learn to distinguish between cultural customs and God's moral absolutes.

Key Verses: Now then, why do you try to test God by putting on the necks of the disciples a yoke that neither we nor our fathers have been able to bear? No! We believe it is through the grace of our Lord Jesus that we are saved, just as they are (Acts 15:10, 11).

Unity does not just happen automatically in the Christian Church. Though there is one Faith, there are many cultures—and sometimes they do clash in seemingly irreconcilable ways. The Rev. Tom Claus, a Mohawk Indian and Christian leader, writes, "The power of the risen Christ has touched people all over the world, whatever their color or background. And just as there are different parts of the human body, all with indispensable functions, so it is with the Body of Christ.

"The American Indians are no exception, but one reason the Indian church has not grown more is that, in the past, Christians have not allowed it to be different. Too often Christianity has become confused with white culture. Older missionaries seemed to believe that these were one and the same. If an Indian was saved, it was assumed he would turn away from all his Indian ways.

"Today, however, we recognize the value of ethnic and cultural differences as part of the search for identity and recognition" (From *Gospel Tidings*, March 1982).

What is your experience with the differences among various cultures? Can you name any examples of ways we are tempted to make our own cultural customs into Scriptural absolutes?

Throughout church history there is a constant tug to add do's and don't's as nonnegotiable items to the Gospel. Alongside the legalists are Christians who shout from the rafters that it is exclusively God's grace through Christ which provides salvation.

This struggle between justification by faith alone or by faith plus works begins in A.D. 49 in Jerusalem. There, the most important church leaders, led by the Holy Spirit, make the right choice in articulating how one becomes a Christian. Often such sticky dilemmas are tied up in a delicate balance of both displaying love and maintaining doctrinal integrity.

Light on the Text

15:1
That "some men" come from Jerusalem indicates they may be on a mission of some kind, but they exceed their responsibilities. These Judaizers are like many well-meaning Christians who believe their opinions are sanctified absolutes. "My way is Yahweh's." Most of us fall into this ego trip at one time or another.

In this situation, these Christians' convictions add works to salvation. They, however, don't perceive it that way. They readily grant that Jesus by His death and resurrection has superseded the place of the traditional system of sacrifices. But in their way of thinking, this does not abrogate other aspects of the Law. With large numbers of uninstructed believers coming into the church, a training program needed to be inaugurated. They argue, "What better program is there than the one designed to prepare an individual for proselyte status?" This includes circumcision, which they teach as a nonnegotiable part of salvation.

15:2a
Under different circumstances, Paul can be expected to affirm the Law. After all, the Old Testament is relevant for our moral conduct. He has no complaint against Jewish Christians who are "zealous for the law" (21:20).

In fact, his policy is "To the Jews, I became like a Jew, to win the Jews . . ." (I Cor. 9:20, 21). But this particular situation makes Barnabas and Paul very angry. It is one thing to encourage Jews to affirm their heritage; it is something else to impose this heritage on Gentiles as part of salvation. Paul doesn't budge an inch on the issue of justification by grace alone.

(Paul's Epistle to the Galatians deals in depth with the conflict between rigid Jewish Christians and Gentile believers. Scholars debate whether the letter is written before or after the Jerusalem Council. We won't go into the arguments either way, but the Bible student will find it helpful when studying Acts 15 to refer to Galatians, particularly chapters 1 and 2.)

15:2b The Antioch church and other Gentile churches are torn apart over this controversy. The dissension sours fellowship and unity. Paul and Barnabas, plus others, are appointed to visit Jerusalem and resolve the question of circumcision.

15:3, 4 Not only do the churches in Phenicia and Samaria rejoice at the spreading of the Gospel among Gentiles, but the Jerusalem church welcomes them and is eager to hear reports. Apparently the Judaizers are not as strong as they insisted in Antioch.

15:5 Acts 6:7 reports that many priests become obedient to the faith. A minority among the Pharisees leads the Judaizers, and they press their grievance to the congregation.

15:6-11 Any Christian who has attended an annual church meeting (or certain committee gatherings) can appreciate the implications of "much discussion" (vs. 7). Each side needs to air its opinions. In this issue, and in those we face, key questions are: What pleases God? What directions do we have concerning His will? Peter eloquently points to experience, recalling how God gave the Holy Spirit to the Gentile believers gathered at Cornelius's home some ten years before. Despite his mistake in dining at Antioch exclusively with the Jewish party (Gal. 2:11-16), Peter is in complete agreement with

Paul: salvation is by grace alone through faith in Jesus. He asks why the Gentiles should try to fulfill laws that have not even given the Jews salvation.

15:12 Obviously, Barnabas and Paul's recounting of their missionary work has the assembly spellbound.

15:13-18 James, brother of Jesus, sums up the meeting and confirms the results with Scripture, using Amos 9:11, 12. ". . . James's application of the prophecy finds the fulfillment of its first part (the rebuilding of the Tabernacle of David) in the resurrection and exaltation of Christ, the Son of David, and the reconstitution of His disciples as the new Israel, and the fulfillment of its second part in the presence of believing Gentiles as well as believing Jews in the Church" (F. F. Bruce).

15:19-21 Although it is clear to James that no stumbling block should keep the Gentiles from salvation, he also believes they should be encouraged to exemplify the godly morals found in Jewish practices. They can learn the Law from synagogue readings, and the Jerusalem church can instruct them in four crucial areas. James is the Christian who will declare, "Faith without deeds is dead" (James 2:26).

15:22 The entire Jerusalem congregation is included in choosing Judas and Silas to represent them and to deliver their letter of encouragement to Antioch.

15:23-29 Although the letter is sent to believers in the province of Syria-Cilicia of which Antioch is the capital, it has a wider audience (see 16:4). It is sometimes called the Jerusalem decree, and can be viewed as a kind of Christian law of purity.

   The four standards are not simply a compromise to appease Jewish sensitivities. Rather, they guard the church against paganism and idolatry. The first rule deals with abstaining from meat sacrificed to idols and made available to the public through a feast or at a butcher's shop. Abstaining would leave no doubt that the believers took seriously the worship of the one, true God. Paul discusses this in I Corinthians 8.

The second rule is given because some cults drank blood as part of their worship. Thirdly, animals strangled (not butchered by bloodletting) were forbidden under Jewish dietary laws. By abstaining from these meats, fellowship with Jewish Christians who practiced the Orthodox diet could be assured. Finally, immorality was a big problem for nonbelievers whose worship often included the use of prostitutes.

15:30-35 The Jerusalem letter encourages the Antioch Christians. Circumcision is not mandated, the other instructions are readily adopted as church policy, and they receive the bonus of being taught by Judas and Silas.

15:36-41 Barnabas and Paul, who have endured so much together, part company after a "sharp" disagreement. They, too, have feet of clay. Luke's account doesn't place blame on either side, and ultimately God directs two missionary teams instead of one. Paul recalls the able teacher Silas from Jerusalem, who also has the advantage of being a Roman citizen (16:21). They travel, via land and through Paul's homeland, to the Galatian cities visited on Paul and Barnabas's first journey. Barnabas and John Mark follow up the churches on Cyprus (Barnabas's homeland) which had also been visited on the first missionary journey."

We may speculate that Paul is right in evaluating John Mark's unreadiness for another tough trip, but Barnabas is right, too, in perceiving Mark's leadership abilities.

Based on both Barnabas's and Paul's emphasis on encouragement and love among brothers and sisters in Christ, we can also assume that they reconcile, perhaps through a letter or messenger, perhaps through John Mark.

16:1, 2 In Lystra (where a year or two earlier a crowd had mistaken Paul for Hermes and went from worshiping him to stoning him) lives a three-generation family of believers, obviously the fruit of Paul and Barnabas's visit. There is grandmother Lois, mother Eunice, and son Timothy (II Tim. 1:5). Timothy receives high commendation from many local "brothers" because of his walk with the Lord.

16:3   Paul wants Timothy to accompany Silas and him, but there is a problem. This son of a Jewish mother and Greek father is by Jewish law a Jew, but also by Jewish law not a Jew, because he is uncircumcised.

Now you may wonder why Paul, who vehemently argued against circumcision in chapter 15, now circumcises Timothy! First, don't confuse "circumcision as a means of salvation with circumcision as a legal act to remove a stigma from Timothy" (I. Howard Marshall). Second, Paul and Timothy's willingness to do this can teach something about facing opposition: when one in good conscience can avoid opposition, one should.

After Timothy's circumcision, the local church sends him out with their blessing. The circumcision will prevent an unnecessary distraction throughout the mission.

16:4, 5   When one thinks of Paul's missionary journeys, one often thinks of his pioneering and planting new churches. Another important aspect of the work, however, was following up and strengthening the churches that had already been started.

For Discussion

1. In what ways does legalism today put an unnecessary yoke on salvation? Can you think of any examples from your own experience or observation?

2. In Biblical interpretation, how do you distinguish between commands that are merely a product of the culture of that day, and those that transcend time and culture?

10

An Example to Follow

Truth to Apply: From Paul's example on his second missionary journey, I can learn practical ways to demonstrate my faith and to be a model for other Christians.

Key Verse: The churches were strengthened in the faith and grew daily in numbers (Acts 16:5).

The apostle Paul, as one of our spiritual ancestors, provides us with an excellent example of the Christian life lived to its fullest in obedience to God's will. He wrote: "Whatever you have learned or received or heard from me, or seen in me—put it into practice. And the God of peace will be with you" (Phil. 4:9).

If you had to choose someone as a "model Christian" (of the past or present), who would it be? Why?

This lesson looks at Paul's deeds during his second missionary journey, and at those faithful saints who follow his example as he follows Christ. They are our spiritual ancestors.

Light on the Text

16:6-10 Paul, Silas, and Timothy have completed follow-up in churches planted during Paul's first journey. Now they want to enter Asia, possibly crossing it to get to the key city, Ephesus, in Asia Minor. We do not know how the Holy Spirit prohibits them, but twice their plans are thwarted.

Entering the port city of Troas, the disciples continue to be open to God's leading. A vision (or dream) shows Paul that north to Greece is the appropriate next step. Here, for the first time, is the use of the first person plural, "we," indicating that Luke, the beloved physician, joins the team. This use continues until 16:17 and returns in 20:5.

16:11, 12 The natural element of wind favors their voyage to Philippi, shortening to two days a 125-mile sea voyage that can take five days (20:6). They dock 10 miles away at the port city of Neapolis.

Luke's description of Philippi as a "leading city" reveals civic pride and suggests he may have been a native. Perhaps he trained at its medical school.

16:13-15 The wealthy businesswoman Lydia, originally from commercial Thyatira in Asia Minor, becomes the first convert in Europe. Lydia immediately offers hospitality to Paul and his party, and shares material goods with those who teach the Word.

16:16-21 In contrast to the pastoral conversion of Lydia, Luke details the exorcism of a young slave who has gifts of ventriloquism and clairvoyance. In the Greek, she is called a "pythoness," one who receives such gifts from the god of oracles, Apollo. The disciples' patience toward the evil spirit's disruptions lasts "many days." Finally, Paul challenges the enemy in Jesus' name, freeing the girl.

The result is that the slave loses her moneymaking value for her masters. The upset owners grab Paul and Silas, apparently ignoring Timothy and Luke, and incite a mob to drag them before local Roman officials.

The accusations don't deal with exorcism, but point to the disciples' Jewishness and their supposedly anti-Roman cult.

"The Romans were officially not supposed to practice foreign cults, although in practice they might do this so long as these did not offend against Roman customs. The principle was clearly a flexible one which could be invoked as necessary" (I. Howard Marshall).

16:22-24
The magistrates by policy are to arrest accused individuals and hold them until a hearing before a higher-ranking proconsul. Submitting to crowd pressure, however, they order Paul and Silas severely beaten (probably 39 lashes with the flagellum—straps of leather tipped with bits of bone and metal) and then throw them into prison.

16:25-30
Paul and Silas must be men of great physical stamina to endure such a beating. Although curses and groans would be the norm, these two courageous men of God pray and sing!

In two prior incidents (Acts 5:18-20; 12:5-11) God released His witnesses from jail through supernatural means.

Paul shows the compassion of a great heart. Just as the jailer's sword flashes in the dim light, he loudly assures him no one has escaped. Surely the jailer had never encountered such cooperative prisoners!

Notice the jailer's inquiry about salvation. He may be asking about his physical deliverance from death (see 12:19); however, he may know something of Paul and Silas's message from their earlier street preaching, or that night he has listened to their testimony in prayer and song.

16:31-34 The disciples challenge the jailer to a personal and intimate trust in the saving mercy of God in Christ. Then they set forth in detail the way of salvation, not just to the jailer, but also to his family.

The words here reflect John the Baptist's command to "bear fruit that befits repentance" (Mt. 3:8, RSV). A vivid expression of repentance at this moment is the jailer's concern for Paul and Silas's wounds. Paul has no doubt about the reality of this conversion. He administers baptism to the jailer and his family.

16:35-40 Does Paul refuse to turn the other cheek? "In Paul's case, there is no question of revenge, but of just treatment according to Roman law. For Paul and Silas to have crept meekly out of jail would have been to acquiesce in the abuse of power displayed by the magistrates. . . . Paul does not demand vengeance for having been illegally beaten—only that the authorities acknowledge their wrong" (*Community Bible Study Commentary*).

Part of Paul's effectiveness is that he moves on to other mission fields while leaving young churches under the leadership of others. Luke's dropping of the first plural, "we," may mean he stays behind.

17:1-9 The missionaries travel to the largest city in Macedonia, Thessalonica, a port city, 100 miles from Philippi. They take the Egnatian Way through Amphipolis and Apollonia.

Paul continues his custom of preaching the Lord first to the Jews. Notice the verbs describing his witnessing style.

Although a few Jews accept the view of a suffering Messiah, the God-fearing Gentiles are again the more responsive group to the Gospel, as are prominent city women. Paul's rapport with these women creates jealousy and desperation in the Jewish leadership. Their frustration is evident: note who they enlist for help!

Jason, a common Greek name for the Jewish name Joshua, becomes the mob's scapegoat since they can't find Paul and Silas. The accusation of Roman treason has just enough truth in it to be used as a deadly weapon; indeed, the Gospel does present a Kingdom as well as the King of Kings.

17:10 Under cover of darkness, Paul and Silas head for Berea, possibly leaving Timothy behind. Berea (modern Verria) is about 60 miles southwest of Thessalonica.

17:11, 12 These Jews and God-fearers give the contemporary Christian an excellent example for discerning what to believe. They ask, "Where is it written in Scripture?" and then eagerly check the sources.

17:13- 15 It doesn't take long for the Thessalonian Jews to realize Paul has not been banished very far. Some of the troublemakers arrive in Berea and use the same mob technique to detract from the Gospel's progress. The text is not clear as to how Paul reaches Athens, but it suggests the Bereans throw the pursuers off the track. Timothy and Silas remain in Macedonia until Paul's new destination is established.

17:16- 18 No city excels Athens in its cultural history. This had been the home of Socrates and Plato, and the adopted home of Aristotle, Epicurus, and Zeno. Many of the Greek artifacts we see in art books come from Athens. Seeing them detached from their pagan significance we can appreciate the craftsmanship, but Paul is "troubled" by the blinding idolatry they represent.

Stoics, with determined jaws, have great confidence in human reasoning power and the ability to live in harmony with nature. Epicureans, with upturned mouths, seek pleasure and the elimination of all fears, including that of death. They view the gods as uninterested in human affairs.

17:19- 21 The Areopagus represents a place on 370-foot-high Mars' Hill, and the council which meets there. The council reviews the rights of teachers who lecture in public, and deals with questions of morals.

17:22 Commentators debate on the success of Paul's eloquent speech to cultured pagans. It resulted in a few converts (vs. 34), but there is no evidence an Athenian church was established. But as Paul's Pisidian Antioch speech illustrates his approach to Jews (13:16-41), this speech and the one at Lystra (14:14-18), demonstrate the apostle's approach to pagans.

17:22, 23	Paul's tone is conciliatory. The "unknown god" altar becomes an object lesson to point to Christ.

17:24-28	Paul challenges the Epicurean notion that the universe comes about by chance. He further counters their view about uninvolved deities by stating God's relationship to Creation. The God of Genesis is a caring Father who expresses His concern for His people through the order of nature. He is not simply a glorified natural force.

Although God is independent of humankind, humankind is not independent of God. Under Him, all people have a common condition of dependency. From one person—the first Adam—all came into being.

"Reaching out" to God suggests a groping in the dark despite His nearness. This may allude to Romans 1, where Paul goes into more detail on humanity's failure to find God.

He next makes a tactical move of no small merit: he quotes two poets the Athenians know. "In him we live . . ." is attributed to the Cretan poet Epimenides. "We are his offspring" is from the *Phaenomena* of Aratus, a popular Stoic poet-philosopher.

17:29-31	Paul argues that people, created in God's image, need to repent of idolatry because it falsely depicts the Creator. His challenge to the Stoics is emphasized in verses 30 and 31. He says that at death humans are not simply absorbed into the essence of the universe as the Stoics teach, but rather will face judgment under "the man he has appointed" (that is, Jesus Christ).

17:32-34	Mention of resurrection produces a reaction of open ridicule and polite put-off. But a few, like Dionysius and Damaris, understand that the message of Christ is true wisdom (I Cor. 1:18-25). Paul spends only three or four weeks in Athens.

18:1   Forty miles west of Athens, on an isthmus, lies Corinth, the capital of the province of Achaia. It was a bustling commercial city with a multinational face. Many were enticed by its immoral practices—including a temple to Aphrodite serviced by 1000 prostitutes. Every two years the city attracted countless athletes, tourists, and merchants for the Isthmian Games, similar in attraction to the modern Olympics. Providing tents for these crowds was a decent way to make a living. Paul enters the city with fear and trembling (I Cor. 2:1-4).

18:2, 3   Scholars disagree on whether Priscilla and Aquila become Paul's converts or already are Christians. The three quickly become friends and co-workers.

    Scribes and Pharisees did not take payment for their teaching, but were self-supporting. Paul makes a living through tentmaking, popular in native Tarsus, and also a trade that includes working with leather goods.

18:4, 5   Paul's teaching is limited mostly to Sabbath instruction until money from the Philippians, through Timothy, frees him to preach exclusively (Phil. 4:15).

    Some scholars suggest that Timothy's report of the persecuted Thessalonian believers inspires Paul to write his first epistle to them from Corinth. This is the last place Silas is mentioned by name in Acts.

18:6-8   Paul shakes out his clothes to rid them of synagogue dust. It symbolizes his break of responsibility for these hardened Jews. In sacrificial generosity, God-fearer Titius Justus offers Paul his home.

    Crispus, one of the few Corinthians Paul baptized (I Cor. 1:14), resigns as synagogue ruler, and he and his family also leave with Paul.

18:9-11   Although Paul's work appears to be going well—or at least no differently than in other places—this is a low point in his evangelistic ministry. His heart often aches for the Jews who hate him (Rom. 10:1). Perhaps he thinks of quitting or moving on. The vision from the Lord gives him needed encouragement, as it will in 23:11 and 27:23.

18:12-17	Scholars use an ancient inscription of Gallio's proconsulship in Corinth (dated A.D. 51) to date the rest of Paul's missionary journeys. Gallio was the brother of the famous orator Seneca, who said of his sibling, "No mortal is so pleasant to anyone as Gallio is to everybody." As proconsul of Achaia, Gallio sets a tolerant precedent for treatment of witnessing Christians.
18:16, 17	Ejected from the court, it seems the Jews vent their frustrations on Sosthenes, a possible Christian sympathizer who later converts (I Cor. 1:1). Another possible interpretation is that the Gentile crowd, expressing anti-Semitic hostilities and seeing Gallio's unconcern, do the beating themselves.
18:18	Gallio's decision allows Paul to finish his work in Corinth. He heads back to the province of Syria, of which Antioch is the capital and home base.

For Discussion

1. Looking at Paul's speech to the Areopagus, do you think he presents the Gospel adequately as an introduction, or should he have taken this one-time opportunity and been more specific? What would you have done?

2. In our own witnessing, must a certain theological groundwork be laid before the Gospel can be presented in detail? Explain.

11
My Brother's Keeper?

Truth to Apply: When faced with difficult choices, I must diligently seek to discern my true Christian responsibility.

Key Verse: I served the Lord with great humility and with tears, although I was severely tested . . . (Acts 20:19).

—You are a company vice-president and discover the president has been embezzling funds. Should you personally confront the president, take the matter before the board of directors, or do nothing?

—You are a checkout clerk at a store and you notice that the clerk next to you is shortchanging customers. Should you speak to the clerk about it, tell the store's management, or do nothing?

—In the mail you receive solicitation for an organization you believe to be engaging in consumer fraud. Should you write a letter of complaint to the organization, contact the Better Business Bureau, or do nothing?

In each of the situations described above, there is room for differing opinions. There may be no single right or wrong answer in a particular case. What are the options a Christian has in confronting such issues? When does faith take a quiet stance, and when does faith take action?

Background/Overview: *Acts 18:18—21:16*

"Responsibility" may be a word we dislike until we contrast it with "irresponsibility." Given the choice, we'd rather be recognized as reliable people than as uncommitted rascals.

This lesson, tracing Paul's third missionary journey, is filled with contrasts between the two choices in behavior. For example, silversmith Demetrius's irresponsibility results in a riot. The foolishness of seven exorcists brings violence upon themselves, whereas the proper use of a prophetic gift by Agabus warns Paul of future trouble.

Light on the Text

18:18 With his work established in Corinth, Paul takes the 1000-mile sea voyage back to Antioch, Syria. He, Priscilla, and Aquila leave through Corinth's east harbor, Cenchrea, where Luke mentions that Paul cuts his hair. "A temporary Nazirite vow (usually 30 days) involved abstinence from alcohol and also from cutting one's hair. Its conclusion was marked by shaving one's hair completely off and offering a sacrifice in the Temple at Jerusalem" (I. Howard Marshall). Hair could be cut off before the vow was fulfilled, but the necessary sacrifice indicates that Paul must visit Jerusalem.

18:19-23 Priscilla and Aquila remain in Ephesus, and despite an encouraging Jewish response, Paul knows it is God's will for him to return home. With prevailing winds favoring Caesarea, Paul lands there.

Luke hastens over the apostle's follow-up work in Galatia and Phrygia. This route will lead him by land to Ephesus.

18:24-28 Well learned, with a receptive heart, Apollos knows that John the Baptist's ministry points to Jesus as the Messiah, and he supports this claim using Old Testament prophecies. Some scholars suggest Apollos learns of Jesus from a Palestinian traveler or even by reading a primitive gospel writing circulating at that time.

19:1-7 The incident that confronts Paul when he arrives at the great commercial seaport of Ephesus is controversial: it is the only incident in the New Testament where people receive a second baptism. Various interpretations have been offered: (1) Some Christians argue that these "disciples" are believers and receive the Holy Spirit in a second baptism. (2) Others say that John the Baptist's followers are not yet believers, but like God-fearers, they live out their faith as far as their knowledge has led them. (3) Still others believe these disciples represent a unique situation during a unique time in the Church's history. Thus their situation as ignorant Christians calls for a special introduction to the Holy Spirit.

19:8-10 Like the strategically located Corinth in Greece, Ephesus in Asia Minor provides Paul with the best opportunities to evangelize—not just this key city but the entire province (vs. 10).

It was the Jews who asked Paul to stay when he visited the first time (18:19, 20). Now their inclination toward hostility grows, until Paul leaves them and uses the lecture hall of teacher Tyrannus. ". . . Paul had the use of the building from 11 a.m. to 4 p.m. Tyrannus no doubt held his classes in the early morning. Public activity ceased in the cities of Ionia for several hours at 11 a.m. . . . and more people would be asleep at 1 p.m. than at 1 a.m. But Paul, after spending the early hours of the day at his tentmaking (20:34), devoted the hours of burden and heat to his more important and more exhausting business, and must have infected his hearers with his own energy and zeal, so that they were willing to sacrifice their siesta for the sake of listening to Paul" (F. F. Bruce).

19:11, 12 It is not surprising that as an apostle Paul does the same mighty works accomplished by Christ and the other apostles (II Cor. 12:12; Rom. 15:18, 19). The handkerchiefs and aprons are actually "sweat rags" in Paul's leather/tentmaking work.

19:13-16	Like Bar-Jesus on Cyprus (13:6), many renegade Jews abuse their religion's reputation and practice magic under it. Sceva's sons, who all participate in an exorcism, meet their match.
19:17-20	The Gospel definitely makes an inroad into paganism here. Genuinely changed people give up professions and old habits. The break can be an expensive one: a drachma is about a day's wages!
19:21, 22	Luke depicts an energetic Paul who desires to return to Jerusalem, to follow-up churches in Macedonia and Achaia, and even to evangelize Rome. Yet, there are strains. Luke mentions these plans prior to the riot to suggest that Paul does not leave because of pressure.
19:23-27	Demetrius is a skillful psychologist. He initiates a trade union meeting and emphasizes not only the fact that Paul's message means no business and no bread, but also threatens local and religious pride. *The Interpreter's Bible* observes that "when devotion to religion and patriotic sentiment can be made to coincide with self-interest, then fanatical intolerance knows no bounds! The whole story is so vivid and so true to life that it is impossible to doubt its historicity."
19:28, 29	R. C. H. Lenski estimates that the commotion of the mob moving their demonstration into the street draws as many as 25,000 people. The silversmiths' chant contains no verb. The cry is literally "Great Diana of the Ephesians!"
19:30-34	The Jews, concerned that the crowd will turn on them because of the Christians, try to explain through spokesman Alexander.
19:35-41	Whereas one man uses oratory to incite a riot, another quells the mob. A city clerk is one who drafts decrees, manages city coffers, presides at citizens' assemblies, and acts as liaison between the people and Roman officials. An astute student of human behavior, this clerk allows the crowd's energy to dissipate before speaking.

20:1-3 Some scholars suggest, on the basis of II Corinthians 2:12-14, that when Paul traveled to Macedonia he went north through Troas. There he searched for Titus, whom he earlier had sent to the troubled Corinthian church with a letter (now lost). Anxious to hear how the Corinthians were doing, he moved farther into Macedonia and found Titus. He then likely wrote II Corinthians, sending it ahead with Titus (II Cor. 8:16-24).

Making his way to Corinth, Paul perhaps also evangelized western Greece (Rom. 15:19). F. F. Bruce says the journey from Ephesus to Corinth took about a year (A.D. 55-56). At Corinth, Paul probably produced the Epistle to the Romans.

His plans to be in Jerusalem by Passover are stymied because of an assassination plot, probably by those who threatened him earlier (18:12-17). He returns by backtracking and doing more follow-up through Macedonia.

20:4, 5 Here is a remarkable list of the fruits of Paul's ministry. It illustrates his dedication to disciple those around him in an intimate way and shows his organizing abilities. These Gentile Christians are his emissaries. They also most likely have been commissioned by their churches to present cash donations to the financially strapped Jerusalem church (I Cor. 16:1-4; II Cor. 8:10-24). For reasons unknown, they travel ahead of Paul to Troas.

20:6 Paul spends an Easter Passover celebrating the perfect Lamb of God with his dear Philippians. The first person plural "we" returns. With Luke now along, more journey details appear.

20:7-12 This is the first direct reference in the New Testament to Christians' meeting on Sunday (see also I Cor. 16:2; Jn. 20:19, 26; Rev. 1:10). F. F. Bruce mentions that the believers meet at night because it is a more convenient time for Gentile believers who are servants.

How many of us can identify with the groggy, young Eutychus? Luke may record this miracle because of his interest as a physician. Once Eutychus is revived, Paul

85

shares Communion and eats a meal, then he continues to teach and encourage until daybreak!

20:13-16	Paul's walk to Assos, a more direct route than by sea, allows him extra time in Troas. The rejoined group then spends an overnight stop at Mitylene, chief city of the island of Lesbos. Their ship passes the islands of Chios and Samos, and docks for a few days at Miletus. Because of his desire to reach Jerusalem for Pentecost, Paul chooses a faster ship that does not dock at Ephesus. However, he sends for the Ephesian elders ("guardians," or "overseers") who live 30 miles away.
20:17-21	Paul's farewell is the only speech in Acts that addresses a Christian audience. It contains many parallels to Paul's recorded thoughts in the epistles. Basically the speech deals with his example and the example the elders are expected to set for the church. Paul is a role model for them. Notice that Paul has not refused to announce the hard parts of the Gospel: its call to repentance, its high call to holiness, its statement of the suffering of Christ to turn aside God's wrath.
20:22-24	At times in Acts we have seen Paul face death without fear (stoned at Lystra, beaten at Philippi). At other times he avoided the possibility of dying (leaving Damascus by night, escaping an assassination plot at Corinth). Notice what is more important to him, even than life or death! Also, Paul indicates that the Holy Spirit sometimes instructs him specifically and at other times guides him as we are guided in our own daily lives. In either case, the Christian life is one of faithful following.
20:25-27	A few scholars theorize that Paul visits Ephesus again despite his sense that this is a final farewell. Paul, however, views his work as completed. The word "kingdom" (vs. 25) emphasizes God's rule in a Christian's heart. "Innocent of the blood of all men" reminds one of Ezekiel 33:6. There, an unfaithful watchman who fails to call the city to defend itself is guilty of the blood of those who die in the resulting debacle. But Paul has given the Ephesians fair warning.

20:28-32 This portion contains exhortation and instruction. Similar to the responsibility of any church's guardians, the responsibility of these Ephesian leaders is to watch out for destruction from without and from within. The latter is usually the more dangerous.

The most pointed words in the address are "which he bought with his own blood" (vs. 28). Literally, the phrase is "by means of blood of His own." Perhaps the "own" refers to God's Own [Son]. Some translations (the RSV, for example) do supply the word "Son" here.

20:33-35 Probably as Paul speaks he holds up calloused hands. Although he rightfully could have accepted a salary, he has a divine compulsion to be self-supporting, allowing someone else's burden to be lifted because of it. Paul's quote of Jesus' famous words are not recorded anywhere else in the New Testament.

21:1-6 After Miletus, the group sails south of the island of Cos and docks at the port of Rhodes a day later. Next they travel east along the south coast of Asia Minor to Patara (or Myra). From there they take a fast ship over 400 miles to Tyre. Because they have made good time, they visit for a week. In verse 4 some Christians, possibly those with the gift of prophecy, confirm Paul's Jerusalem premonition.

21:7-11 Another 40 miles, with an overnight at Ptolemais, and they reach Caesarea, home of Philip the evangelist (6:5; 8:1-40) and his four daughters—all prophets. Yet it is another prophet, Agabus (11:27), who symbolically wraps himself with Paul's outer garment and declares the trouble awaiting Paul. "We are to understand the several prophetic forecasts not as prohibitions from the Holy Spirit but as forewarnings of what lay ahead" (*Wycliffe Bible Commentary*).

21:15, 16 Finally Paul's journey concludes in Jerusalem.

Mnason is a Hellenist Jew who either provides hospitality for Paul and his Gentile believers somewhere between Caesarea and Jerusalem, or he is their host in Jerusalem.

For Discussion

1. Even though we understand people will act to protect business and social interests (like Demetrius and friends), what responsibility do Christians have to challenge vested interests that clearly stand in opposition to the Gospel and to human development?

2. Look through the temptations that limit service in this lesson. Identify one that prevents you from serving others effectively. Are there ways other class members might help you become more released to serve? Are there ways you might help them?

12
God and Caesar

Truth to Apply: Paul's example provides me with a frame of reference for dealing with governing authorities in my life.

Key Verse: Then Agrippa said to Paul, "Do you think that in such a short time you can persuade me to be a Christian?" (Acts 26:28).

"Dad, I know you're not going to believe this, but Alex was arrested today!"

It was enough to jolt Bob out of his chair. *Oh, no,* he thought. What kind of trouble had his foolhardy nephew gotten himself into now?

"Whatever for?" gasped Bob.

"Alex and I and the other Students for Peace were protesting at the grand opening of ANGRA, a big government contractor that builds nuclear warheads. They said we were trespassing, and called the police. The cops came and they hauled away Alex and four other people. They're to spend the night in jail."

Bob felt his face turning red. Her smugness really disturbed him. "Young lady, breaking the law is never right. You know as well as I do what Paul says in Romans about submitting to the law. It's as simple as this: If you disobey the government's law, you're disobeying the law of God. Is that what you want to do? Defy what the Scriptures say?"

"Dad, do you really think that's what Paul was saying? Do you really think he meant we should *always* obey the government?"

Do you agree with Bob's statement that we should always obey the law? Use Bible passages to defend your answer.

Background/Overview: *Acts 21:17—26:32*

This lesson covers almost one-fifth the Book of Acts, but don't panic. It's fast paced and action packed. Surprisingly, unlike the rest of Luke's narrative, we will not read of any transformed lives, except that of Paul, whose testimony reappears twice. What Luke gives us is a picture of an innocent, always witnessing Christian, aptly contending with governing authorities. There are some rather interesting characters, but the star performers are the apostles, and the Lord who stands nearby (see 23:11).

Light on the Text

21:17-19 It had probably been five years since Paul had visited Jerusalem. By now the original 12 disciples were either dead or evangelizing outside of Jerusalem. James, Jesus' brother, is the able leader of the local church, along with the "elders," estimated by F. F. Bruce to be about 70 men. They give the apostle a warm reception.

21:20-22 False reports of Paul's work among the Gentiles, however, have created suspicion. Jewish believers have heard that he advocated abandoning Jewish culture and laws.

21:23-25 The elders propose that Paul participate with four poorer church members, who have taken a Nazirite vow. It is hoped Paul's example will silence rumors circulating within the local church. How unfortunate that this should be necessary!

21:26 Some liberal commentators do not believe Paul would so readily accept the elders' plan, based on how adamantly he defends Jesus as the fulfillment of the law (see Rom. 2:25-30). Paul, however, makes himself a servant to all that he may win as many as possible (I Cor. 9:19).

21:27-29	It is ironic that in his intent to honor his Jewish heritage Paul is accused of defiling the Temple. The Jews from Asia, most likely Ephesians like Trophimus, are in Jerusalem as pilgrims with thousands of others for the Feast of Pentecost.

First, they illegally seize Paul; then they yell as if murder is being committed before them. John Calvin paraphrases them: "Our religion totters on the edge of destruction!" Look at how they misrepresent Paul's ministry among the Gentiles and make preposterous claims. These charges are successful crowd agitators. Their specific, but unfounded, charge is that Paul earlier brought Trophimus into the Temple's forbidden zone. |
21:30	The sudden collection of people from throughout Jerusalem is like what happens to children on a school playground when someone shouts "Fight!" The phrase at the end of this verse means they shut the doors with a bang and at once. What doors? The ones between the inner courts where only Jews worship and the outer, Gentile court.
21:31, 32	From the Tower of Antonia, built in the northwest corner of the wall surrounding the Temple, Roman soldiers quickly respond to the commotion. Two or three hundred men rush into the courtyard, their presence temporarily intimidating the mob.
21:33-36	That Paul is bound with chains suggests the Romans believe they have a seditious man. This act fulfills Agabus's prophecy (21: 10, 11).
21:37-40	Assuming Paul is an uneducated Jewish scoundrel, the commander is surprised that Paul knows the popular trade language, Greek. Then he asks, hoping it's his lucky day, if Paul is the Egyptian terrorist who is high on their "most wanted" list.
22:1-20	Throughout his testimony, Paul uses words and phrases tailored for Jewish ears. This is the second of three accounts in Acts that recall Paul's testimony (9:1-31; 26:1-23). The main theme points to God as the director

of Paul's activities. Verses 17 and 18 contain an interesting detail of God's warning Paul, through a vision, to leave Jerusalem.

22:21-23   Mentioning Gentiles in any favorable light infuriates the crowd. "God's commission to Paul seems to call into question the uniqueness of Israel as God's people, to deny the saving efficacy of the Law, and to attack Jewish reverence for the temple and all its rituals" (*Community Bible Study Commentary*). The Jewish focus on self-preservation and ethnic pride keeps them from fulfilling their calling to be a light to the Gentiles.

22:24-30   The commander probably does not understand Paul's Hebrew speech and now resorts to torture to uncover the cause of the disturbance. Flogging with the flagellum often resulted in death or permanent crippling. Its use is not permitted on a Roman citizen, at least not until found guilty by trial.

In verse 28 the commander is either sarcastically saying Roman citizenship has lost its value since it can be purchased with money, or he understands its value since he has paid a high price to obtain it. Paul responds that his citizenship has been earned as an inherited right.

23:1-3   As Paul makes his defense, the high priest Ananias orders him struck. With passion and indignation, Paul rebukes Ananias for hypocrisy. We can either allow that Paul loses his temper or that his prophetic consciousness comes to expression here. He speaks out against the corruption of the Jewish leaders as Christ did.

23:4, 5   Despite Ananias's poor reputation, those in the Sanhedrin rebuke Paul's disrespect of the office he represents. Why doesn't Paul recognize the high priest? Some commentators reason he has poor eyesight—that he responds only to Ananias's voice coming from a group of priests. Others believe he speaks in irony that such an unjust order comes from a high priest. Paul recognizes his error, quoting Exodus 22:28.

23:6-9   Since Paul quickly realizes that a fair hearing is impossible, he appeals to the Pharisees. In verse 9 these teachers of a resurrection declare his innocence. When they ask "What if a spirit or an angel has spoken to him?" they probably refer to Paul's mention of visions in his earlier speech.

23:10, 11	Though Paul has had a potentially disheartening night in jail, he is uplifted by an encouraging affirmation from the Lord. He will get his desire to go to Rome.
23:12-15	What hatred Paul experiences because of his obedience to God! Forty frustrated men either must have starved to death or lived with an unfulfilled vow!
23:16-22	Part of a Roman citizen's prison rights included visitation privileges. Somehow Paul's nephew finds out about the ambush plot and reports to the apostle. "When Paul says in Philippians 3:8 that for Christ's sake he has 'suffered the loss of all things,' it is usually inferred . . . that he was disinherited for his acceptance and proclamation of Jesus as Messiah. . . . But it appears that the mother of the young man retained some sisterly affection for her brother, and something of that affection had been passed on to her son" (Bruce).
23:23-33	Claudius Lysias takes no chances: 470 armed Romans can certainly handle 40 fanatical Jews. Under ordinary circumstances, Luke would not have seen this letter to Felix. Possibly, using his historical skill, he recomposes what had been written. The letter conforms to the accepted style for such documents. Notice that Lysias's message is an accurate account except for a diplomatic twist.
23:34, 35	Although Paul's home, Tarsus, is located in Cilicia, Felix decides to judge what appears to be a minor case rather than sending Paul and his accusers on a long journey north.
24:1-9	The Sanhedrin opponents obtain the lawyer Tertullus to present their case in proper Roman style. After flattering Felix, an accepted rhetorical device, Tertullus presents three charges going from general to specific. Paul is called a worldwide rioter, a ringleader of a sect, a defiler

of the Temple. Look at this last charge in verses 6, 7. Tertullus attempts to justify the disturbance by creating the impression that the Sanhedrin has prevented Paul from desecrating their Temple. With the absent Asian Jews obviously without proof of their charges, the Sanhedrin presents a charge less easily proven or disproven.

24:10-21 Paul also begins with complimenting Felix, but in a less verbose fashion. Unlike Tertullus's generalizations, he pinpoints exactly what he has and has not done in Jerusalem. He strives to show that as a Jewish believer he cannot disconnect himself from Judaism. Verse 15 is one of the few places in the New Testament where Paul declares a resurrection of the wicked as well as the righteous.

24:22, 23 Felix diplomatically postpones a decision. It makes sense that Lysias can provide helpful information, yet in a few verses we learn Felix never decides the case (vs. 27). He appears curious about Jesus' followers. Their reputation obviously has reached him in his five years as proconsul at Caesarea and, prior to that, his four years of office in Samaria.

24:24-26 Perhaps Drusilla, Felix's third wife, is the reason Felix retains Paul at first. A Jewess less than 20 years old, she knows Christians have intrigued her family since her great-grandfather had to contend with the baby in Bethlehem. But when Paul visits with this couple, he does not soft-pedal what they need to hear. His conversation concerns righteousness, self-control, and judgment (compare vs. 15). Felix backs off but keeps Paul in prison, hoping his many Christian connections will cough up a bribe (vs. 17).

24:27 Little is known about Paul's two years in the Caesarean prison from about A.D. 57 to 59, although it appears he has privileges, and Felix talks often with him (vs. 26).

Under Felix's governance of Judea, relations between Gentiles and Jews deteriorate to such a point that Felix is recalled to Rome. This partly explains why he unjustly leaves Paul in prison.

25:1-6 Little is known of Festus, who replaced Felix, and died in office in A.D. 62. We see he desires to do political housecleaning as soon as he assumes his new office, spending time with Jewish leaders in Jerusalem shortly after arriving at the provincial capital, Caesarea. Paul's reputation obviously has not died in prison. The Sanhedrin wants this man tried on its turf—in Jerusalem. Festus wisely remains cautious.

25:7-12 Concerning Roman justice, Festus probably thinks it is inconsequential whether Paul is tried in Caesarea or Jerusalem. But Paul understands the possible implications.

Paul's appeal to Caesar is legally permissible if the proconsul agrees. This decision gets Festus off the Sanhedrin hot seat, and Paul receives a free ticket to the city of his dreams.

25:13-27 Whereas Festus represents Roman power in Judea, Herod Agrippa (A.D. 27-100) symbolizes Jewish power to Rome. Of course, his kingly puppet position is more fluff than stuff, but nevertheless he is royalty. Sister Bernice accompanies him as consort. They both are great-grandchildren of Herod the Great. Since Agrippa knows Jewish culture and laws, Festus discusses Paul's case with him (vss. 19, 20).

26:1-23 This is the third account of Paul's testimony (see 9:1-31; 22:1-21). Here, he zeroes in on Agrippa's Jewish mind. His concern is evangelism as well as defense.

26:24 Festus, unfamiliar with Scripture and the Jewish culture Paul refers to, interrupts when Paul speaks of the resurrection. He is certain Paul has swayed from his defense.

26:25-27 Paul responds politely, but doesn't allow himself to get sidetracked. To further establish the reality of his statements, he claims Agrippa can validate his facts. He pivots back to the king, using a "fishhook" statement to draw him into his closing appeal: "Do you believe the prophets? I know you do."

26:28, 29   This king cannot deny the prophets unless he wants to alienate the support of the religious leaders, yet he cannot accept Paul's reasoning of Jesus as the Messiah. F. F. Bruce suggests that Agrippa's oblique response, apparently designed to lighten Paul's earnest plea, best translates, "In short [time] you are trying to make me play the Christian." Paul's final plea in verse 29 expresses the genuineness of his witnessing.

26:30-32   Enough has been discussed. The king adjourns this meeting. He and Festus realize that Paul's innocence should have brought a ready acquittal, except for the technicality that he has appealed to Caesar. Now he must go to Rome.

For Discussion

1. Can you find examples in this lesson where God's will is woven into the events and activities of others, even non-Christians? What does this teach about the will of God in our lives?

2. Does Paul's example offer guidelines as to how to respond to governing authority in your life? Since you are a citizen of the heavenly Kingdom, what obligations do you have as a citizen of an earthly kingdom?

13

Strength to Go On

Truth to Apply: In times of crisis, I have access to spiritual resources that do not fail me.

Key Verse: For I have faith in God that it will happen just as he told me (Acts 27:25).

The older we get, the more we realize that life is neither problem free nor predictable. As English journalist Malcolm Muggeridge puts it, life is drama. Sometimes life's plot includes scenes we would have rather seen discarded in the playwright's circular file. The first-century Christians probably felt this way about more than a few crises they had to deal with.

In your own life, what has been the key to handling life's crises? How well have you done? In what ways would you like to improve in your ability to persevere faithfully?

In this lesson Paul receives his share of suffering, but he allows God the opportunity to bring grace to the crises he experiences. Through these hardships his relationship with God becomes richer. "Not only so, but we also rejoice in our sufferings, because we know that suffering produces perseverance; perseverance, character; and character, hope. And hope does not disappoint us, because God has poured out his love into our hearts by the Holy Spirit, whom he has given us" (Rom. 5:3-5).

Light on the Text

27:1, 2   In vivid detail Luke describes Paul's extremely dangerous journey to Rome. Throughout the story, God's protection blankets His loved ones. Imagine the apostle in chains, constantly watched by a Roman soldier, and attended by companions like Luke and Aristarchus (20:4; Col. 4:10; Philem. 24). Supervising Paul's delivery to Caesar is the centurion Julius, who commands other soldiers and prisoners. Paul obtains passage on a grain ship that heads north, docking at many coastal ports.

27:3   Sidon is 70 nautical miles north of Caesarea. Its church was probably founded after Stephen's martyrdom (11:19). Paul's Roman citizenship and stature allow him privileges the average prisoner would not receive.

27:4   The ancient ship, which could not sail against the wind, moves east and north of Cyprus rather than south and west. "The lee of Cyprus" means the side of the island most protected from wind.

27:5   "The Adramyttium ship crept on from point to point up the Asia Minor coast, taking advantage of every opportunity to make a few miles, and lying at anchor in the shelter of the winding coast, when the western wind made progress impossible" (W. M. Ramsay, *St. Paul the Traveller*).

27:6-8	Julius finds one of the grain ships from Alexandria, Egypt, and the group's new ship presses on with difficulty: past Cnidus, a port on the southwest tip of Asia Minor; continuing in the lee of Crete, or the south side of this island; and on to a poor winter harbor on Crete, Fair Havens.
27:9	First-century sailors traveled at great risk due to hazardous and unpredictable winds between September 14 and November 11. After those dates, shipping activities halted altogether until early February. F. F. Bruce and other scholars the "Fast," or "Day of Atonement," when Jews collectively repent of their sins, fell on October 5th in A.D. 59.
27:10-12	Some commentators question why Paul, a prisoner, confers readily with the ship's decision makers. He is, however, an experienced traveler and a "holy man," even in pagan eyes. But the majority overrules his advice. Phoenix, farther west on Crete, offers a much better winter harbor.
27:13-16	It is easy to miss how treacherous the events of this story are. The "Northeaster," a walloping storm, comes up suddenly and pushes them out to sea for 14 days. There is no rest from jostling, seasickness, dampness, and the fear of death.
27:17	The lee of the island of Cauda, 23 miles from Crete, provides a temporary, but still stormy, respite. The crew can now bring aboard the water-filled lifeboat (in calm waters it trails behind the larger vessel); undergird the ship with cables to keep it from breaking apart; lower the anchor to act as a brake against wind and waves.
27:18, 19	More drastic measures to lighten the ship (now filling with water) include throwing cargo overboard (vs. 18), and later, the tackle or spare equipment (vs. 19).
27:20-22	When morale reaches the point of despair, Paul begins a speech that sounds like a rather obnoxious "I told you so." Actually, he is simply being straightforward. He was

right then, and he is right now in telling them they will live despite the circumstances.

27:23　This confidence does not make Paul conceited. His message doesn't imply "Here's Paul and here's Paul's God." His words focus his listeners' attention on God rather than himself: "Here's God ('of whose I am') and here's God's Paul." The angelic message is not so much a new promise as a reassurance of what Paul had been promised earlier (see 23:11 and 26:15-17).

In these three passages, which deal with Paul's commission to the Gentiles, we see an important principle illustrated: God's promises are not given apart from a purposive *chain of promise.* Just as there is one basic promise in Paul's life, on which all other promises are elaborations, so there is one basic promise in Scripture, on which all other promises depend. The *promises* of God must be understood in light of the *promise* of God (II Pet. 3:9; Heb. 10:36-39). The God of history has promised and given one gift—the Deliverer. All lesser promises make sense only when they relate to Him. (This idea is borrowed from Willis J. Beecher's *The Prophets and the Promise,* Baker Book House.)

27:24　In view of the preceding comments relating God's promises to Christ, why do you think God "graciously" spares all 276 passengers on Paul's ship?

27:27-32　The sailors' sensitive ears hear waves hitting against a shoreline. In the darkness, with the mixed hope of land as safety and its danger of crushing their ship against its rocks, some sailors attempt escape. Because of Paul, the soldiers hamper the plan. There will be no doubt the rescue is under God's hand.

27:39-44　On Melita, modern-day Malta, there exists a bay, now called St. Paul's Harbor, which fits the geographical description for this miraculous rescue. Just as Paul predicted, despite almost 500 miles of stormy weather, the sailors' attempt to escape, and the soldiers' plan to execute the prisoners, everyone makes it to shore. In spite of the sudden and dramatic changes of fortune, Paul's hope is in the unfailing Word of God.

28:1-6 Malta lies 60 miles south of Sicily. The natives speak a Phenician dialect instead of Greek. This language barrier is why some Bible translations call them "barbarians." Their kindness to the shipwrecked passengers is unexpected.

In verse 4 the superstitious islanders assume that a god named Justice has caused a poisonous snake to bite Paul because Paul managed to escape the punishment of death by shipwreck. When Paul shows no side effects, the islanders believe *he* is a god! Their quick change of opinion is told in such a way as to reflect Luke's "quiet humor" (F. F. Bruce). Some commentators believe that Mark 16:18, which refers to protection from snakebites, alludes to this incident.

28:7-10 Although Luke mentions no conversions on Malta, he leads us to understand that Paul's three months there are taken up with the usual facets of his ministry. That the Greek text refers to Publius as "chief" official is one of the many details in Acts showing Luke's concern for accuracy: this title has been found on two ancient Maltese inscriptions.

28:11-13 Other ships are spending the winter months on Malta. Centurion Julius finds another vessel from Alexandria whose figurehead, a sailor favorite, symbolizes good fortune in a storm. Once the group sets sail, they probably reach Syracuse, on Sicily's east coast, in one day. Next they sail to Rhegium, an important harbor in the toe of Italy. From there they easily make it to Puteoli, part of the Bay of Naples and the principle port of southern Italy.

28:14, 15 Paul's seven days in Puteoli are probably due to the centurion's need to do other business there. This stopover allows news of his arrival to reach Rome ahead of him. Christians from the Forum of Appis (40 miles outside of Rome) and the Three Taverns (over 30 miles from Rome) greet him and accompany him on the Via Appia, the road to the city of Caesar.

Obviously, Paul's spirit has been down. Luke says their reception makes him thankful and encouraged.

Sometimes we regard too lightly the encouragement and strength our brothers and sisters in Christ can give us, or we them. God meets Paul's needs through these people, but they have to be willing to walk the 40 miles each way to be used by Him.

28:16   Further encouragement occurs through Roman arrangements for Paul to live under house arrest rather than in prison. He still must be handcuffed to a soldier, but ministry has greater possibilities.

28:17-20   Paul initiates interaction with Rome's Jewish leaders. He presents his case, not emphasizing mistreatment at the hands of the Jerusalem Jews, but summarizing the events that have brought him to their city as a prisoner. He stresses, as he always does to Jewish hearers, that his message is not an attempt to sabotage the Jewish faith. Rather, Jesus is the fulfillment of the prophecies and the Jewish hope.

28:21, 22   The Jewish leaders profess open-mindedness, which is commendable if they are sincere. They have heard the Christian sect criticized from all sides, but no news has reached them from Jerusalem headquarters. (Perhaps the Sanhedrin dropped pursuit once Paul was away from their shores.)

28:23   What a day this must have been! From morning until evening Paul expounds, testifies, and persuades. He doesn't give a one-hour lecture, but a careful, thorough, systematic presentation. There is surely much dialogue, questioning, and exploring of texts from the Law and Prophets. Paul's theme is not new: the Kingdom of God and the name of Jesus Christ have been the focus throughout Acts.

28:24-29   Some accept what Paul says, and some do not. To those who reject his message, he proclaims that they, too, are fulfilling prophecy. He quotes the same text Jesus used to describe the Jews who refused to allow His words to penetrate their hearts. The passage was given to Isaiah when he first became a prophet and was warned that people would not welcome God's Word (Isa. 6:9, 10).

Paul declares that, likewise, the Jews have not accepted God's *Logos*. Their ears are unalert. Their eyes are closed as if they are afraid they might see something that will make them change their firmly held, comfortable convictions.

John writes that Jesus "came to that which was his own, but his own did not receive him" (Jn. 1:11). But as heartbreaking as this fact is, John continues, "Yet to all who received him, to those who believed in his name, he gave the right to become children of God" (Jn. 1:12). Such is the experience of Paul and the other disciples: they experience rejection but offer the Good News to whoever will accept it.

28:30, 31 Although Acts ends without our knowing the conclusion of Paul's trial, it leaves the reader with the impression of a Christian doing what he loves best: boldly explaining how God's Kingdom focuses on Jesus Christ—dead, buried, resurrected, and coming again.

But what happens after Paul's two years under house arrest? Commentators' opinions vary. Although Paul's time of death remains uncertain, tradition holds that he was acquitted at the end of Acts, did further missionary work (perhaps including Spain), was arrested and imprisoned a second time in Rome, and finally was executed by the sword. Perhaps just prior to execution was when he wrote to Timothy: "For I am already being poured out like a drink offering, and the time has come for my departure. I have fought the good fight, I have finished the race, I have kept the faith. Now there is in store for me the crown of righteousness, which the Lord, the righteous Judge, will award to me on that day—and not only to me, but also to all who have longed for his appearing" (II Tim. 4:6-8).

Tradition has it that Luke did not survive long after Paul's death, possibly suffering martyrdom in Greece. Of him, scholar E. M. Blaiklock summarizes, "He is an accurate, and able historian, and has left some of the most powerful descriptive writing in the New Testament. . . . Luke must have been a person of singular sweetness of character to earn the apostle's adjective 'beloved' (Col. 4:14). He is obviously a man of outstanding loyalty, of unusual capacity for research, and the scholar's ability to strip away the irrelevant and dispensable detail" (*Pictorial Bible Dictionary*).

For Discussion

Review your study of Acts and write down several important concepts you have learned about your relationship with God, and God's relationship with the Church. Share how they apply to your life right now.

Leader Helps and Lesson Plan

General Guidelines for Group Study

*Open and close each session with prayer.

*Since the lesson texts are not printed in the book, group members should have their Bibles with them for each study session.

*As the leader, prepare yourself for each session through personal study (during the week) of the Bible text and lesson. On notepaper, jot down any points of interest or concern as you study. Jot down your thoughts about how God is speaking to you through the text, and how He might want to speak to the entire group. Look up cross-reference passages (as they are referred to in the lessons), and try to find answers to questions that come to your mind. Also, recall stories from your own life experience that could be shared with the group to illustrate points in the lesson.

*Try to get participation from everyone. Get to know the more quiet members through informal conversation before and after the sessions. Then, during the study, watch for nonverbal signs (a change in expression or posture) that they would like to respond. Call on them. Say: "What are your thoughts on this, Sue?"

*Don't be afraid of silence. Adults need their own space. Often a long period of silence after a question means the group has been challenged to do some real thinking— hard work that can't be rushed!

*Acknowledge each contribution. No question is a dumb question. Every comment, no matter how "wrong," comes from a worthy person, who needs to be affirmed as valuable to the group. Find ways of tactfully accepting the speaker while guiding the discussion back on track: "Thank you for that comment, John, now what do some of the others think?" or, "I see your point, but are you aware of . . . ?"

When redirecting the discussion, however, be sensitive to the fact that sometimes the topic of the moment *should be* the "sidetrack" because it hits a felt need of the participants.

*Encourage *well-rounded* Christian growth. Christians are called to grow in knowledge of the Word, but they are also challenged to grow in love and wisdom. This means that they must constantly develop in their ability to wisely apply the Bible knowledge to their experience.

Lesson Plan

The following four-step lesson plan can be used effectively for each chapter, varying the different suggested approaches from lesson to lesson.

STEP 1: *Focus on Life Need*

The opening section of each lesson is an anecdote, quote, or other device designed to stimulate sharing on how the topic relates to practical daily living. There are many ways to do this. For example, you might list on the chalkboard the group's answers to: "How have you found this theme relevant to your daily life?" "What are your past successes, or failures, in this area?" "What is your present level of struggle or victory with this?" "Share a story from your own experience relating to this topic."

Sharing questions are designed to be open-ended and allow people to talk about themselves. The questions allow for sharing about past experiences, feelings, hopes and dreams, fears and anxieties, faith, daily life, likes and dislikes, sorrows and joys. Self-disclosure results in group members' coming to know each other at a more intimate level. This kind of personal sharing is necessary to experience deep affirmation and love.

However you do it, the point is to get group members to share *where they are now* in relation to the Biblical topic. As you seek to get the group involved, remember the following characteristics of good sharing questions:[1]

1. Good sharing questions encourage risk without forcing participants to go beyond their willingness to respond.

2. Good sharing questions begin with low risk and build toward higher risk. (It is often good, for instance, to ask a history question to start, then build to present situations in people's lives.)

3. Sharing questions should not require people to confess their sins or to share only negative things about themselves.

4. Questions should be able to be answered by every member of the group.

5. The questions should help the group members to know one another better and learn to love and understand each other more.

6. The questions should allow for enough diversity in response so each member does not wind up saying the same thing.

7. They should ask for sharing of self, not for sharing of opinions.

STEP 2: *Focus on Bible Learning*

Use the "Light on the Text" section for this part of the lesson plan. Again, there are a number of ways to get group members involved, but the emphasis here is more on learning Bible content than on applying it. Below are some suggestions on how to proceed. The methods could be varied from week to week.

*Lecture on important points in the Bible passage (from your personal study notes).

*Assign specific verses in the Bible passage to individuals. Allow five or ten minutes for them to jot down 1) questions, 2) comments, 3) points of concern raised by the text. Then have them share in turn what they have written down.

*Pick important or controversial verses from the passage. In advance, do a personal study to find differences of interpretation among commentators. List and explain these "options" on a blackboard and invite comments concerning the relative merits of each view. Summarize and explain your own view, and challenge other group members to further study.

*Have class members do their own outline of the Bible passage. This is done by giving an original title to each section, chapter, and paragraph, placing each under its appropriate heading according to subject matter. Share the outlines and discuss.

*Make up your own sermons from the Bible passage. Each sermon could include: Title, Theme Sentence, Outline, Illustration, Application, Benediction. Share and discuss.

*View works of art based on the text. Discuss.

*Individually, or as a group, paraphrase the Bible passage in your own words. Share and discuss.

*Have a period of silent meditation upon the Bible passage. Later, share insights.

STEP 3: *Focus on Bible Application*

Most adults prefer group discussion above any other learning method. Use the "For Discussion" section for each lesson to guide a good discussion on the lesson topic and how it relates to felt needs.

Students can benefit from discussion in a number of important ways:[2]

1. Discussion stimulates interest and thinking, and helps students develop the skills of observation, analysis, and hope.

2. Discussion helps students clarify and review what they have learned.

3. Discussion allows students to hear opinions that are more mature and perhaps more Christlike than their own.

4. Discussion stimulates creativity and aids students in applying what they have learned.

5. When students verbalize what they believe and are forced to explain or defend what they say, their convictions are strengthened and their ability to share what they believe with others is increased.

There are many different ways to structure a discussion. All have group interaction as their goal. All provide an opportunity to share in the learning process.

But using different structures can add surprise to a discussion. It can mix people in unique ways. It can allow new people to talk.

Total Class Discussion

In some small classes, all students are able to participate in one effective discussion. This can build a sense of class unity, and it allows everyone to hear the wisdom of peers. But in most groups, total class discussion by itself is unsatisfactory because there is usually time for only a few to contribute.

Buzz Groups

Small groups of three to ten people are assigned any topic for discussion. They quickly select a chairperson and a secretary. The chairperson is responsible for keeping the discussion on track, and the secretary records the group's ideas, reporting the relevant ones to the total class.

Brainstorming

Students, usually in small groups, are presented with a problem and asked to come up with as many different solutions as possible. Participants should withhold judgment until all suggestions (no matter how creative!) have been offered. After a short break, the group should pick the best contribution from those suggested and refine it. Each brainstorming group will present its solution in a total class discussion.

Forum Discussion

Forum discussion is especially valuable when the subject is difficult and the students would not be able to participate in a meaningful discussion without quite a bit of background. People with special training or experience have insights which would not ordinarily be available to the students. Each forum member should prepare a three- to five-minute speech and be given uninterrupted time in which to present it. Then students should be encouraged to interact with the speakers, either directly or through a forum moderator.

Debate

As students prepare before class for their parts in a debate, they should remember that it is the affirmative side's repsonsibility to prove that the resolve is correct. The negative has to prove that it isn't. Of course, the negative may also want to present an alternative proposal.

There are many ways to structure a debate, but the following pattern is quite effective.

1. First affirmative speech
2. First negative speech
3. Second affirmative speech
4. Second negative speech
(brief break while each side plans its rebuttal)
5. First negative rebuttal
6. First affirmative rebuttal
7. Second negative rebuttal
8. Second affirmative rebuttal.

Floating Panel

Sometimes you have a topic to which almost everyone in the room would have something to contribute, for example: marriage, love, work, getting along with people. For a change of pace, have a floating panel: four or five people, whose names are chosen at random, will become "experts" for several minutes. These people sit in chairs in the front of the room while you and other class members ask them questions. The questions should be experience related. When the panel has been in front for several minutes, enough time for each person to make several comments, draw other names and replace the original members.

Interview As Homework

Ask students to interview someone during the week and present what they learned in the form of short reports the following Sunday.

Interview in Class

Occasionally it is profitable to schedule an in-class interview, perhaps with a visiting missionary or with someone who has unique insights to share with the group. One person can take charge of the entire interview, structuring and asking questions. But whenever possible the entire class should take part. Each student should write a question to ask the guest.

In-Group Interview

Divide the class into groups of three, called triads. Supply all groups with the same question or discussion topic. A in the group interviews B while C listens. Then B interviews C while A listens. Finally C interviews A while B listens. Each interview should take from one to three minutes. When the triads return to the class, each person reports on what was heard rather than said.

Following every class period in which you use discussion, ask yourself these questions to help determine the success of your discussion time:

1. In what ways did this discussion contribute to the group's understanding of today's lesson?

2. If each person was not involved, what can I do next week to correct the situation?

3. In what ways did content play a role in the discussion? (I.e., people were not simply sharing off-the-top-of-their-head opinions.)

4. What follow-up, if any, should be made on the discussion? (For example, if participants showed a lack of knowledge, or misunderstanding in some area of Scripture, you may want to cover this subject soon during the class hour. Or, if they discussed decisions they were making or projects they felt the class should be involved in, follow-up outside the class hour may be necessary.)

STEP 4: *Focus on Life Response*

This step tries to incorporate a bridge from the Bible lesson to actual daily living. It should be a *specific* suggestion as to "how we are going to *do* something about this," either individually, or as a group. Though this is a goal to aim for, it is unlikely that everyone will respond to every lesson. But it is good to have a suggested life response ready for that one or two in the group who may have been moved by *this* lesson to respond *this week* in a tangible way.

Sometimes a whole group will be moved by one particular lesson to do a major project in light of their deepened understanding of, and commitment to, God's will. Such a response would be well worth the weeks of study that may have preceded it.

Examples of life response activities:

1. A whole class, after studying Scriptural principles of evangelism, decides to host an outreach Bible study in a new neighborhood.

2. As a result of studying one of Paul's prayers for the Ephesians, a group member volunteers to start and oversee a church prayer chain for responding to those in need.

3. A group member invites others to join her in memorizing the key verse for the week.

4. Two group members, after studying portions of the Sermon on the Mount, write and perform a song about peacemaking.

Obviously, only you and your group can decide how to respond appropriately to the challenge of living for Christ daily. But the possibilities are endless.

---

[1]From *USING THE BIBLE IN GROUPS*, by Roberta Hestenes. © Roberta Hestenes 1983. Adapted and used by permission of Westminster Press, Philadelphia, PA.
[2]The material on discussion methods is adapted from *Creative Teaching Methods*, by Marlene D. LeFever, available from your local Christian bookstore or from David C. Cook Publishing Co., 850 N. Grove Ave., Elgin, IL 60120. Order number: 25254. $14.95. This book contains step-by-step directions for dozens of methods appropriate for use in adult classes.